Polynesia

Vincenzo Berghella

Copyright Page

Copyright year: 2016

ISBN No: 978-0-578-18586-6

From the same author:

- **Obstetric Evidence Based Guidelines.** Informa Healthcare, London, UK, and New York, USA (2007) [English]

- **Maternal Fetal Evidence Based Guidelines.** Informa Healthcare, London, UK, and New York, USA (2007) [English]

- **Laughter, the best medicine. Jokes for everyone.** (2007) [English]

- **Ridere, la migliore medicina. Barzellette per bambini.** (2007) [Italiano]

- **My favorite quotes.** (2009) [English]

- **In medio stat virtus – Citazioni d'autore.** (2009) [Italiano]

- **Quello che di voi vive in me.** (2009) [Italiano]

- **Dall'altra parte dell'oceano.** (2010) [Italiano] (Translated in: **On the other side of the ocean.** (2013) [English])

- **Preterm Birth: Prevention and Management.** Wiley-Blackwell. Oxford, United Kingdom. (2010) [English]

- **From father to son.** (2010) [English]

- **Sollazzi.** (2010) [Italiano]

- **The land of religions.** (2011) [English] (Translated in: **La terra delle religioni.** (2013) [Italiano])

- **Giramondo.** (2011) [Italiano]

- **Obstetric Evidence Based Guidelines.** Informa Healthcare, London, UK, and New York, USA (2012; Second Edition) [English]

- **Maternal Fetal Evidence Based Guidelines.** Informa Healthcare, London, UK, and New York, USA (2012; Second Edition) [English]

- **Trip to London.** (2012) [English]

- **Il primo amore non si scorda mai**. (2012) [Italiano]

- **Maldives.** (2013) [English]

- **Russia.** (2013) [English]

- **Happiness: the scientific path to achieving wellbeing.** (2014) [English] (Translated in **Felicita': il percorso scientifico per raggiungere il benessere** [Italian])

- **New Zealand: 100% pure.** (2014) [English]

- **Me dentro: i primi scritti dai 17 ai 20 anni** (2015) [Italiano]

- **Me dentro: alla ricerca dell'amore** (2015) [Italiano]

- **US Rowing Youth Nationals** (2015) [English]

Dreaming

When I was a child, there was nothing to me more exotic than Polynesia. I would look at a world map, and be attracted by the huge expanse of the Pacific, with these islands looking like tiny drops of sand spotted on the circled globe. Micronesia, Polynesia: synonyms of far-away lands, of exotic places, of the unknown.

Paola loves the beach, and tropical places. Bora Bora had been her dream since we met. In 2013, when she turned 50, we had in mind to go to Bora Bora for spring break 2014. But after studying the possibility a bit, Paola figured that the weather may be rainy in March, and so we eventually opted for the Maldives.

This year we came up with a more democratic and involved system. By brainstorming, Paola, Andrea, Pietro and I came up with 9 possible destinations. And then we each secretly voted from 1 to 10 our most to least favorite ones. The Galapagos came in first, followed by Fiji, Australia, Seychelles, Spain, etc.

So we started exploring the many possibilities of a Galapagos vacation. I figured Paola would love it as she adores animals. And the kids actually took a school class on Darwin in January 2016, and have always been interested in Evolution. The flight to Quito was actually fairly easy, and relatively cheap.

The problem came when Paola realized that this had to be a boat trip. To visit the Galapagos once one lands there, you have to visit them by ship. And the thought of a week on a vessel for someone who can have seasickness like Paola became suddenly very unappealing.

As we started exploring Fiji and other possibilities, the thought came back to the old love: what about another Pacific island, like Bora Bora? This year actually the kids have 2 weeks (!!) of spring break, so we could stay more than the usual week. Paola checked the weather in French Polynesia again: while the dry season starts in April, the rainy season is mostly December through February.

So leaving for example around March 19 would get us there closer to April than February, closer to a drier season than not. It was a gamble. Going so far and getting pouring rain would not be fun. But we had really no other choice. Spring break is always in this time of the year.

The travel guides were clear. Seasons in the Society Islands (which include Bora Bora, Tahiti and Moorea) follow fairly predictable patterns. November-February is rainy, warm and humid and typhoon season. Though not many typhoons hit the area, this is the highest probability time. Runoff from the mountains especially on Tahiti and Moorea can cause muddy waters at some dive sites.

March – May is pleasant with generally calm seas and fairly good visibility. Water temperatures which were up in the mid 80's in January are beginning to cool. June-August brings the coolest water temperatures meaning upper 70's to around 80 but the best visibility. It also brings the wind and choppier sea conditions. September and October are great months to dive. Visibility is still good, temperatures are just beginning to rise and the humpback whales are in season. Often you can hear their magnificent calls and see them breeching off the island of Moorea.

We got to the internet, and slowly found places to stay, and flights. It's a bit stressful to book flights before hotel, or vice versa, but we got a good idea of where to stay first, and then booked flights and soon after hotels. We are going to French Polynesia! Excitement is all in the preparations, and these were major ones.

March 19, 2016

Over 40 years have passed since my childhood dream. I'm now on the plane from Philadelphia to Los Angeles, and the next one will be from Los Angeles to Pape'ete. Pape'ete is the capital of Tahiti, the biggest island of French Polynesia. A dream is about to become reality.

I've made the trip from the US East Coast to the US West coast probably close to one hundred times now. I've always lived on the East coast, either in New York or Philadelphia, for now an incredible 32 years. Averaging about three times a year for East-West coast trips (last year I did them three times just between February and April 2015), the math adds up.

In 1996 we went to Hawaii for a conference, and had an incredible experience, in a wonderful land. Two years ago I was lucky enough to fly from Los Angeles to Auckland, in New Zealand. What a wonderful, adventurous trip. But I've never been in the 'middle' of the Pacific Ocean.

In fact, if one looks at this largest of oceans on a map, and puts a finger in the middle, where in low definition there appears to be nothing but water, that's where in fact the tiny islands of French Polynesia hide. This is a trip to the middle of nowhere. Civilization and the main continents are far, far away.

While I write, my wife Paola sleeps, as usual on a long plane ride. Andrea naps, just like his mother. They are twins, really, so similar in anatomy and in so many personality traits. Pietro is restless, just like his father (me!).

His girlfriend, Gabby, is actually flying with us. When Gabby weeks ago heard from Pietro we were going to Bora Bora, her mother Lori got all exited as this was a dream of theirs, too.

As we had already met and liked Gabby's mother and father, a few email exchanges between Lori and Paola did the trick. They were able to book pretty much the same flights, and the same hotels. So on this plane from Philadelphia to Los Angeles, Pietro, a lanky 6'6", 16 year old sophomore, is standing and talking to extremely beautiful 5'4", blonde blue-eyed Gabby. She's flawless. Love is a wonderful thing. But he loves her more (as he says as a running theme between them).

We four Berghella's are traveling light. We have just five carry-ons, but one of them we check in since it has liquids, in particular lots of strong sun lotions, like 30 or 40 or 50 SPF. The carry-ons otherwise are full of bathing suits, t-shirts, polo shirts, sport shorts and Bermuda shorts. Even Paola has just a carry-on.

Our first American Airlines flight is at 6:05pm, and should get us to LAX at 9:21pm. The second flight is on Air France and is scheduled to leave at 12:55am from LAX and arrive at 6:25am in Pape'ete, Tahiti, French Polynesia.

I'm very excited about this trip. As usual, for me the best part of traveling is the months and weeks before, organizing it, dreaming it, learning a bit about the new places. I have a wonderful Lonely Planet travel guide that I've read and now re-read again, trying to memorize the highlights.

Andrea and I have time to go to the VIP lounge, so he can have a clean bathroom – same needs as his mother ☺. We also get some free food and drinks, and I read a bit of the Economist, always a wonderful source of international information. I bring back some cookies for the group.

I just can't believe we are going to Bora Bora, in French Polynesia. It seems too good to be true. Do I deserve this? Really?

French Polynesia is made up of 118 islands. French Polynesia is an 'overseas collectivity' of France, or collectivité d'outre-mer de la République française (COM). It is sometimes unofficially referred to as pays d'outre-mer (POM). Its islands and atolls stretch over a huge expanse of more than 2,000 kilometers (1,200 mi) in the South Pacific Ocean – this is almost as large an area as Western Europe!

French Polynesia – Polynesia means 'many islands', from the Greek - total land area is about 4,167 square kilometers

(1,609 sq mi) – this is just about 30% bigger than the US state of Rhode Island, or less than half the size of my native Italian central region of Abruzzo.

French Polynesia is divided into five groups of islands: The Society Islands archipelago composed of the Windward Islands and the Leeward Islands; the Tuamotu Archipelago; the Gambier Islands; the Marquesas Islands and the Austral Islands.

The Society Islands are to the west, with Tahiti and Moorea to the east being some of the Windward Islands, and Bora Bora and others being the Leeward Islands. The Australs, as the name says, are to the south. The Gambier archipelago is straight east from the Australs, hundreds of miles away. Above the Gambier archipelago, there are the Tuamotus islands, at about the same longitude as the Society Islands. A few hundred miles north of the Tuamotus, there are the Marquesas Islands.

Interestingly, Tahiti is more French, Bora Bora has an American feel because of the GIs leaving there in the 1940's, the Australs and the Tuamotus have British influences, while the Gambier Archipelago and the Marquesas are more French. The Tuamotus are where the French did the nuclear explosions in the 1970's.

Among French Polynesia's 118 islands and atolls, 67 are inhabited. 'High islands,' for example Tahiti, Moorea and Bora Bora, the ones we are visiting, are essentially volcanic mountains rising out of the ocean, encircled by a barrier reef. A protected shallow lagoon with usually turquoise waters forms between the reef, which often comes out of the ocean floor, and the volcanic island.

An atoll instead is a ring of coral barrier reef that surrounds a now sunken island. Over time these atoll or island reefs can build up above the water level. The coral reef then often forms motu – which means islets. These motu which encircle either the present or now-absent island in the middle, reach a maximum height of only a few meters, like 2-6. They are usually covered with coconut trees and low bushes.

Motu are separated by very shallow channels, often not navigable. These are called 'hoa.' When these channels get deep enough and large enough to allow the passage of boats, they are called a 'pass.'

Tahiti, which is located within the Society Islands, is the most populous island and the seat of the capital of the collectivity, Pape'ete. This city has more than 68% of the population of the islands. That is where we are headed first.

Our first flight from Philadelphia to Los Angeles goes very well. As we disembark at LAX, Pietro notices that his carry-on is no longer in the overhead compartment. Someone must have taken it mistakenly, probably having a similar bag. As we wait at the exit of the airplane, we inform the land stewardess, who is not very friendly. She says we cannot go back in the plane, but she will.

She later comes back without our missing carry-on. As the last passengers, ten long minutes later, are still disembarking (we were some of the first ones out, sitting in rows 6 and 7), a black lady with two kids comes back to the gate saying she took the wrong bag (hers was similar to ours and the stewardess had found it above our seats), and she gives back our bag. This is what happens when you have a black anonymous bag. We are obviously relieved!

We walk for quite a while to the international terminal. We go through long lines to get through security. The planes boarding from this part of the airport all go to exotic places, like Manila, Doha, Melbourne, Auckland, Hong Kong, Tokyo, etc. I ask the kids to name the nation where these cities are from. Jake is the quickest to answer for most of them.

Once close to our gate, we have dinner with the Schwartz's very freely, casually. They are wonderful people. Henry Schwartz, the father, is a lawyer, originally from Pittsburgh. He reminds me a lot of my dear friend Don Korkis. He is really a gentleman, very altruistic, always puts others first. His hands move the same as Don's, incredible.

Lori is beautiful, tall, refined, a true lady. She is also very polite, well-mannered, American royalty. Their son Jake, a 17-year-old junior at Andrea and Pietro's school, Germantown Friends School, is a blond blue-eyed (like everyone in the family) quiet but wonderful guy, gregarious. I'll have great times with him throughout the trip.

Of course we know Gabby the best. She has been dating Pietro since about October. They are madly in love with each other. They always hold hands, or touch each other in some way. She is really stunningly beautiful, long blonde wavy hair, light blue eyes, a ready smile, perfect features.

So as I was saying, at LAX airport we all grab some food. I have again some Chinese, like I did in Philly. The four kids share a table as far away from us four adults as possible. Henry is really nice and buys some liquor to take on the trip. Paola waits forever for her quesadillas.

Our Los Angeles – Pape'ete flight is on Air France. One already begins to feel outside the US. We board at 1am, and take off a bit late. We are all really tired, and soon fall asleep. Pietro finds a way to sit near Gabby, and stays with her the whole flight. I sleep next to Paola, who is also next to Andrea.

March 20, 2016

We all sleep about 5 or 6 of the 8 hours from Los Angeles to Pape'ete, the capital of Tahiti. There is significant "turbulence" – pronounced almost unintelligibly, as the stewardess keeps announcing in French through our sleep. The Air France flight is overall pleasant though. Seats are not super small. As the flight takes off at about 1:20am LA time, which is about 4:20am for us, we were plenty tired, ready to sleep.

I wake up a bit hungry. The omelet breakfast is warm, and abundant. Through the faraway plane windows a bright red and orange sunrise over the Pacific Ocean illuminates my eyes. There are a few minutes before landing, so I keep on reading the travel guide.

French Polynesia as we know it today was one of the last places on Earth to be settled by humans. Scientists believe the Great Polynesian Migration happened around 1500 BC as Austronesian people went on a journey using celestial navigation from Taiwan or South-East Asia to find islands in the South Pacific Ocean. The first islands of French Polynesia to be settled were the Marquesas Islands in about 200 BC. The Polynesians later ventured southwest and discovered the Society Islands around AD 300.

Any fauna that could not swim, fly or float to Polynesia has been introduced. These first humans brought in their canoes chickens, pigs, dogs and plants. There were no animals in Polynesia other than fish and birds before these Asians arrived. Interestingly, the further east and away from Asia one gets in French Polynesia, the less varied the fauna becomes.

The first Polynesians therefore did not come from South America, as Thor Heyderdahl had claimed. Nonetheless, South Americans did come here at some point. For example, the sweet potato arrived in the Marquesas in AD 300. The Peruvian word for this vegetable is kumar; the Polynesian word is kumara.

Recorded European communication began in 1521 when Portuguese explorer Ferdinand Magellan, sailing in the service of the Spanish Crown, sighted Puka-Puka in the Tuamotu-Gambier Archipelago. But the true 'discovery' of French Polynesia began in the second part of the 1700's.

It seems that explorers from all the main European powers of the time visited the islands of French Polynesia, on several occasions. British explorer Samuel Wallis visited Tahiti in 1767, killed many Polynesians here, and claimed this island for England, naming it 'King George's land.'

French explorer Louis Antoine de Bougainville visited Tahiti the year after, in 1768, and claimed it for France, not knowing Wallis had already been there. British explorer James Cook visited in 1769. In his second expedition to Tahiti, Cook picks Omai, a native, and brings him back to Europe. Omai is the first Polynesian to visit Europe, and becomes a popular socialite. In 1772, Dutchman Jakob Roggeveen came across Bora Bora in the Society Islands.

In 1772, the Spanish Viceroy of Peru Don Manuel de Amat ordered a number of expeditions to Tahiti under the command of Domingo de Bonechea who was the first European to explore all of the main islands beyond Tahiti. A short-lived Spanish settlement was created in 1774 and for a time some maps bore the name Isla de Amat after Viceroy Amat. Bonechea died in Tahiti during his visit, and so ended the Spanish influence in Tahiti.

When Wallis arrived, he assumed the island's chief was Pomare I. Pomare in fact controlled most of Tahiti by 1803, when he died. His son Pomare II took over that year. The Pomare family continued for a few generations to provide the Polynesian leaders, with less and less powers as the Europeans gradually took complete control of these islands. The Pomare's still consider themselves the royal family of French Polynesia.

In 1787-90 the famous true story of the mutiny of the boat, Bounty, happens. Captain Bligh had been sent to Tahiti in 1787 to collect tree samplings of breadfruit and to take them to the Caribbean. His trip takes over 10 months. His crew remains in Tahiti then for over 6 months, as the breadfruit trees were not in season.

Three weeks after they set sails for the Caribbean, on April 28, 1889, Captain Bligh is overturned by Fletcher Christian, his first mate, and his mutineers. They set the captain adrift with eighteen faithful members of the crew on a small boat.

The mutineers return to Tahiti. Many, such as Fletcher Christian, were motivated to reunite with their Polynesian lovers. About 16 of them stay in Tahiti. A few of them instead, including Fletcher Christian, set off for Pitcairn Island, afraid of a possible attack by England once they got the news of the mutiny.

Amazingly, Bligh makes it alive across the Pacific in a 5823km and 41 day voyage which takes him to Timor, in southeast Asia. By 1790 he gets to England. There an inquiry clears him of negligence, and generates a punitive expedition back to Tahiti against the mutineers.

So in 1790 the British do arrive in Tahiti, and round up the mutineers there. They never find instead the Pitcairn mutineers. The odd Tahitian-British colony still present in Pitcairn Island is one of the last vestiges of the descendants, and of the British Empire influence in French Polynesia.

This story will generate a book, Mutiny on the Bounty, in 1932, by Charles Nordhoff and James Norman Hall. Three Hollywood movies will follow: 'Mutiny on the Bounty,' in 1935, starring Charles Laughton as Captain Bligh and Clark Gable as Fletcher Christian. Then another 'Mutiny on the Bounty', in 1962, starring Trevor Howard as Bligh and Marlon Brando as Christian. Here Brando falls in love with his Tahitian co-star, and eventually moves to French Polynesia. The last movie on this story is 'Bounty,' with Anthony Hopkins as Bligh and Mel Gibson as

Fletcher Christian. I make sure we watch this movie as a family about a week before our trip.

Before the Europeans' arrival, Polynesians were polytheistic, worshipping atua (gods) such as Ta'aroa (god of creation), Tu (man god), Tane (god of craftsmen), 'Oro (god of war), and Hiro (god of thieves and sailors).

Christian missions began with Spanish priests who stayed in Tahiti for a year. Protestants from the London Missionary Society settled permanently in Polynesia in 1797, first in Tahiti. Traders and whaling ships began to be seen more often around this angle of the South Pacific.

Up to this point, in the very early years of European influence in Polynesia, the British clergy were the unofficial colonial power. The Pomare kings, allied with the British, were still in place in the Society Islands, the Australs, and the Tuamotus. The French missionaries were instead in control of the Gambier Archipelago since 1834, and the Marquesas since 1838.

So these early days were dominated by an undeclared war of European missionaries from different countries. When in 1836 two French missionaries from the Gambier Archipelago were quietly dropped off in Tahiti, they were promptly arrested and deported by the British. This deportation was considered a national insult by the French.

Eventually French Rear Admiral Dupetit-Thouars arrived in 1842 with the ship La Reine Blanche, gunned Pape'ete from it, and took power from the Pomare kings and the British missionaries. The French took over the islands and established a French protectorate they called Etablissements des français en Océanie (EFO) (French Establishments/Settlements in Oceania).

Polynesian Queen Pomare IV pleaded for British intervention, but to no avail. She was first forced out by the French, but returned to Tahiti in 1847, and stayed as a figurehead. She died in 1877. Her son Pomare V succeeded, but abdicated in 1881, and eventually drank himself to death in 1891.

In 1891, postimpressionist painter Paul Gauguin sails from France to French Polynesia, and settles in the Marquesas in 1897. He dies there of syphilis in 1903 at the age of 54.

In 1946, the EFOs became an overseas territory under the constitution of the French Fourth Republic, and Polynesians were granted the right to vote through citizenship. In 1957, the EFOs were renamed French Polynesia. There are riots in Pape'ete. Pouvana a a Oopa, leader of the separatist movement, is exiled to France.

In 1961, Faa'a International Airport is opened in Tahiti, and thus, the tourism industry takes off.

Since 28 March 2003, French Polynesia has been an overseas collectivity of the French Republic under the constitutional revision of article 74, and later gained, with law 2004-192 of February 27, 2004, administrative autonomy. Two symbolic manifestations of this autonomy from France are the title of the President of French Polynesia and its designation as an overseas country.

We land safely and smoothly in Tahiti. The traveling has been easy so far. In fact, I do not even feel tired. I slept well, and the thrill of being so far away, in this paradise, sprinkles me with adrenaline. We step off the plane on the runway, and the air is soft, warm, the sun is shining. The four of us are all smiling. So are the Schwartz's.

We know we have a close connection in Pape'ete, as we arrive at 6:20am, and our Air Tahiti Pape'ete-Bora Bora flight is at 8am. We have no idea how big Faa'a Pape'ete international airport is. We are a bit afraid not to make the next plane. We Berghella's pass the customs as last passengers, as we do not have the right forms. We find finally our only checked-in carry-on red bag at baggage claim.

Soon we realize the airport is really small. Nobody really checks our bags, as there is little to no security. Right after baggage claim, we see the national flights part of the airport, which is a small area with only three gates, looking out on the runways.

We are greeted by warm air, smiles, many greetings of 'Iaorana'!' ('hello' in Polynesian).

It's only a few minutes after 7am, we made it to the gate! Polynesians in local costumes are singing our welcome. We have plenty of time to catch our third and last flight, the one that will finally take us to our destination, Bora Bora.

Bora Bora is part of the Leeward Islands, still part of the same Society Islands archipelago as Tahiti, which is instead in the Windward Islands of this archipelago. Bora Bora is located 280 kilometers northwest of Tahiti, at 16 45' W. Bora Bora supported Pomare in his push for supreme power over Tahiti. Bora Bora resisted becoming a French protectorate – established in Tahiti in 1842 – until the island was annexed in 1888.

The original name of the island is Pora Pora, which means in Polynesian 'first born.' This name was given because according to local mythology Pora Pora was the first island drawn out of the ocean by the gods, after the creation of Havai'I (Raiatea).

The name was changed from Pora Pora to Bora Bora by the US GIs when they came in 1942 to set up a military base to protect against a possible Japanese attack through the Pacific. The Japanese had already successfully invaded the Philippines, and were threatening Australia. This American World War II strategic move was called operation Bobcat.

In fact, the letter 'b' does not even exist in Polynesian. But the US military, as has happened so many times in history, mispronounced 'Pora Pora' and changed the name. This should be a familiar story to anyone who knows a bit of history, for example about what happened to so many last names of immigrants coming through Ellis Island.

About 6,000 American soldiers came to this island in December 1942. An aviation runway 2,000 meters (6,562 ft.) long was built on the motu most North, Motu Mute. This is the most useful remnant of that American 'invasion,' as it is now the only airport in Bora Bora. Eight massive artillery guns were also installed, and seven of them can still be seen around the island.

The retreat of the Japanese from the Pacific and their eventual defeat in 1945 caused the eventual departure of the US military forces in 1946. Even if the US did try to retain Bora Bora as an American territory from the French, which were obviously in shambles after World War II. But for once, the Americans did not flex their muscles and left Bora Bora to the French, as part of French Polynesia.

The flight to Bora Bora is perhaps the most beautiful short flight I've ever taken. The views are amazing. As there are no seats assigned, and we get in line late, I end up sitting next to a nice-looking young girl from North Carolina, going to Bora Bora for some kind of survival show, called Dating Naked, for VH1. We chat during the whole 45-minute flight, while gazing at the beautiful scenes coming through the airplane windows. Occasionally I get Paola, sitting just in front of me, involved in the conversation.

We pass over Moorea, and then, 280km north-west from Tahiti, comes Bora Bora into view. We spot its south-east tip, where we think our resort is. And then we head past it, to curve back around the west coast of the island in a north direction, as the airport in on the motu most north of the island. We actually fly way past Bora Bora, then turn right and back south towards the runway, which runs north-south. This must be one of the most unique and spectacular runways in the world, on an islet motu!

Just 4 miles long and 2.5miles wide, Bora-Bora consists of a palm-covered barrier reef of semi-connected motus (islets) encircling a deep lagoon. The blue and greens of the water are fantastic. In the middle of the island, the tombstone-shaped 2,379-foot high Mount Otemanu. A landmark. Its peak is pretty much always covered by white clouds, as Paola will notice several times during the trip.

As I'm in the last row and in the aisle seat, I'm the first to step off the twin propeller plane. I can't believe there are still helical airplanes around. This one actually looks pretty new.

Maybe it's better to have twin propeller planes in this part of the world, instead of jets. Who knows.

The heat invades my body. The sun burns my retinas. I love bright light. It gives me life. The four of us take a quick family picture on the runway. We left the Schwartz's in Tahiti, as they have a 10am flight, but we plan to reunite soon.

The airport sits already in paradise. All around us small islands covered in sundrenched coconut palm trees. The sea is turquoise, perfect, glimmering in the bright sun. In the back of the airport, we see what to me is a luxurious yacht, a big white catamaran, waiting to take us to the main island, from Motu Mote. We take more pictures on top of the yacht, especially of the small islet in front of us. It has just one palm tree in it, and a tiki (religious) statue of an ancient, fat, Buddha-like Polynesia goddess.

We take a wonderful 15-minute boat trip from the airport to the harbor in Vaitape. This is the main port, and main settlement in Bora Bora. It's really still a tropical village, with a couple of banks, a school, and a couple of official buildings to remind us, remotely, of civilization. The shops are mostly just shacks, as are the houses, like everywhere else around this island.

There is no McDonalds. No Starbucks. No bank with a recognizable name. No mall. No main grocery store. No postal office I can see. Around the island I spot only one tiny gas station (Total, of course, we are in France after all). We are away from capitalism and commercialization. Only a couple of CocaCola signs on top of some bar shacks pretend to possibly be advertisement, but there is really none. No billboards. All is refreshingly still uncontaminated by the dollar.

Bora Bora is about 38 square kilometers big (or small I guess we should say). Bora Bora was formed by many volcanic eruptions that began about four million years ago, and continued for hundreds of thousands of years. Later we would be taught how the whole island is really a crater, which is obvious only looking from the lagoon towards certain sides of the island.

The tallest point is Mt Otemanu, with his height of 727 meters. Otemanu means 'sea bird,' according to Teuira Henry, author of Ancient Tahiti. Everything is luscious and green. It's beautiful that the shape of this small mountain changes as we cruise around this north-west side of Bora Bora. Next to it is the square peak of Mt Pahia, 661-meter high. This volcanic island now is slowly sinking.

This basaltic, volcanic main island is surrounded, for 360 degrees all around, by the coralline barrier reef. There are only a few breaks in these circular reefs. The barrier reef is now covered with palm trees, and in fact often real long thin islands (motu), even growing to a few feet above sea level, are formed.

We get picked up by a big Polynesian guy who drives our van to the Maitai hotel. Maitai means 'Bon' in French, or 'Good' in English. We are by now sweating profusely. We still have on long-sleeved shirts, and long cotton pants. I think that today it's supposed to snow in Philadelphia. Here we are in tropical paradise.

The Maitai is situated in the southern part of the island, on the famous Matira Bay, well known for its soft white sand and dazzling blue lagoon. Set into the side of the mountain, the rooms offer panoramic views of the motu emerging from the coral reef. On the lagoon side, traditional bungalows afford direct access to the beach, and for those who are over-water, a glass "laguna-scope" floor table allows you to admire the multi-colored coral fish directly from your bungalow.

The hotel is really nice. Nothing fancy, but really tropical, starting from the Polynesian check-in girls. They have us sit down in the reception area, surrounded by lush tropical trees and vegetation. The kind Polynesian girls who staff the check-in put a necklace of fresh, wonderfully-smelling flowers around our heads. In every new hotel we'll arrive in French Polynesia, we receive necklaces of flowers on arrival, and of small seashells on departure.

We are offered right away also fresh juice, it must be a mix of pineapple and mango perhaps. On the side of this lush tropical garden, the Haere Mai restaurant will offer us every morning breakfast. The beach restaurant Tama'a Maitai is open all day and is where we'll have dinner with the Schwartz's later tonight. The Maitai Polynesia on Bora Bora was the first hotel in French Polynesia to earn the EarthCheck Silver certification, recognizing its efforts in sustainable and responsible tourism operations.

As it is only before 10am, our ocean bungalows are not ready. They might not be ready until check-in time, the nice Polynesia lady at the counter says with a shy friendly apologetic smile. That is 2pm. But she does offer for us to use the showers and bathrooms there, close to the reception area.

Of course, to try to befriend the staff right away, I start talking with the reception lady, asking information, history, options there at the Maitai. I keep on eyeing her belly, beautifully circled, looking I'd guess about 24-26 weeks pregnant at least. But when I point to her belly and say, "Baby?" she replies with a smile, "No, no baby." I can't believe what I just did. And I TEACH not to ask a lady if she is pregnant. Now I'm afraid they'll give us the worst bungalows on the resort. Well, they should.

These are the first Polynesians we interact with a bit. Science tells us the first Polynesians arrived in Bora Bora around 900 AD. So recently!! The oldest remnants of humans in French Polynesia are in Raiatea. I'll notice during these splendid days in the Society Islands that many Polynesian women have indeed bellies that make them look pregnant. But I make sure to never ask again!

The heat is unbearable with clothes on, so I change right away. I put on just a bathing suit, and flip-flops. It will be my dress code for 95% of the rest of the trip. The others slowly follow my example. Eventually we leave our entire luggage by the reception, and walk to the beach, just across the street on the other side of the hotel main entrance.

At the Maitai hotel, we have free use of snorkeling equipment such as mask, snorkel and fins, but Paola brought three masks already. We'll use kayaks, and beach towels. For now, we lay down a second on the white lounge chairs, relaxing on the private beach. We go soon in the crystal clear, light blue lagoon waters, and swim a bit. Now I feel better!

The excitement is so much that we have forgotten we should be tired and jet lagged. 11am here is 2pm in Los Angeles, and 5pm in Philadelphia. And actually 11pm in Italy. Wow. We are really on the other side of the world. Even if we did not pass, only by a little bit, the time zone. Interestingly, they never have daylight saving hours here in Polynesia.

We get the rooms much earlier than expected at around noon. They are just about 50 yards further along the lush tropical gardens by the beach, going south. Despite my despicable performance with the kind reception Polynesian lady, we get the two best overwater ocean bungalows in the hotel!! Numbers 105 and 106. Overlooking the south-east, with so much light over our balconies.

Created and designed exclusively for French Polynesia in the 1960's, the overwater bungalows have become the ultimate experience for a stay in these islands. They are indeed dreamy. Our rooms are large and air-conditioned. There is a floor window, with fish swimming happily below. The bathrooms have just a sliding door, with a nice size shower. The bed is large and confortable. The lighting is perfect.

But the best part is the large balcony. In it, there are two super-confortable huge lounge chairs. There is a dock from where one can easily jump into paradise. And an outside shower. I'll use mostly outside showers in Bora Bora. I love showering outside. I'll even jump from the high wooden railing into the blue lagoon the next day.

Most impressive even, though, is the view. Directly in front of us, a motu, with in it the Sofitel Bora Bora Motu Private Island bungalows to remind us we are in paradise. To our right, the coastline and then the bungalows of the Intercontinental Hotel. In between, before the horizon, the white broken waves of the coral reef. On the far left, again the white sand of the coastline, a few boats, and then the Sofitel Marara, where the Schwartz's will be staying. From our bungalows you can see also far a bit on the left the islands of Tahaa and Raiatea.

There is no internet reception anywhere. My cell phone does not have any connection, so no phone service, no messaging, no internet, no WhatsApp, no Facebook, etc. There are two free desktops with internet connection near the concierge, where Andrea and Pietro during our stay in Bora Bora keep us in connection with the rest of the world, and with the Schwartz's.

Then we walk over to the Sofitel Marara. It's only about 250 meters up the road. On the way, we see a Pizza and Crepes place, practically never open. There is a supermarket, Tiare Market, which instead will be extremely helpful. It's really hot, tropical; we have lush vegetation on our left and stunning shoreline on out right. Marvel all around us.

Their hotel is much more upscale and elegant than ours. A real gem. The bar/restaurant is right on the beach, with an infinity pool, and great outdoor seating, with stunning views of the lagoon. The name of this Sofitel, Marara, means Flying fish, apparently a common Polynesian fish. This luxury hotel was built in 1977 by Italian filmmaker Dino de Laurentiis to house Mia Farrow and the crew while filming the movie Hurricane.

We find the Schwartz's at the restaurant having lunch. It's already late, past 2pm or so. As they are almost done, and there is really no space to add extra huge armchairs for the four of us next to them, we move a bit further, closer to the infinity pool, and we sit at an empty table. We are hungry, and so we have a wonderful lunch.

I have Salad Nicoise, my favorite. It reminds me of when I had it in Malaysia. It is so good! Lots of melted tuna, anchovies, and great lettuce and vegetables. It hits the spot big time. While the other Schwartz's go back to their rooms to relax, Henry sits next to us, and we chat. He is so nice, kind, friendly.

We walk back to our hotel probably after 4pm. But in reality I'm just making up these times. I have no sense of time. During this whole vacation, I seldom have the iPhone with me, since it's practically useless here. I'm also afraid it's going to end up in the water, or wet somehow.

Back at our wonderful bungalows at the Maitai, we swim off our balconies. It's amazing that we have coral all below our water residencies, especially below Andrea and Pietro's bungalow. There are so many fish, of beautiful colors, swimming peacefully around the thick columns holding our ocean homes off the lagoon crystal waters.

We realize we have heaven right with us; there is nothing else we need. Paola's masks come very handy. The water is warm, a wonderful temperature, all day and night long, certainly even this long peaceful evening. Our bodies recharge with the healing salty waters caressing us. We are all smiles.

It is great to just relax on the balcony. The lounge chairs are SO confortable. The view is stunning. A postcard could not be designed better. The lagoon waters in front of us, as the sun starts to slowly come down, take hundreds of different hues of blue. Past the railing, peace, beauty, imagined marine life, light, life. I'm fascinated by this wonderland.

Polynesians had no written language, so there is no record of French Polynesia history before the first Europeans arrived and started reporting what they saw. The Society Islands were a kingdom. The population was made up of fishermen, farmers, and servants. Marae were temples of worship. Human sacrifices, as well as infanticide, were not uncommon. These were happy populations, uninhibited by showing their emotions, and sex was a natural part of everyday life.

Even now, our guide says that an accidental pregnancy is more of a blessing than a course. The family is open arms. Adopted children are considered the same as biologic children. Domestic violence and incest are not rare, perhaps linked in some cases to alcoholism.

The fact that mostly naked girls would approach in a very friendly manner the foreign ships coming to these island since the 1700's and 1800's – as we saw in the movie Mutiny on the Bounty

- may have been due to the fact that Tahitian priests would incite them to become pregnant by the strangers to capture their essence, so to eventually have more power over them.

A lot of early historic events after European settlements revolved around religion. French Catholic missionaries arrived on Tahiti in 1834; their expulsion in 1836 caused France to send a gunboat in 1838. In 1842, Tahiti and Tahuata were declared a French protectorate, to allow Catholic missionaries to work undisturbed. Today, Christianity is the main religion of the islands: a majority (54%) belong to various Protestant churches and a large minority (30%) are Roman Catholic.

In the XIX century the way of life in Bora Bora remained traditional, with a bit more development of the two export crops of copra and vanilla. During this period, visiting sailors and traders brought disease, alcohol and guns. The local Polynesian population decreased by about 60% by 1900 mainly due to the introduction of infections they had no immunity to.

The population of Tahiti was estimated around 40,000 in 1760. In 1800 it was estimated at 20,000. In 1820 it was only 6000. Even worse, the population in the Marquesas went in one century from 80,000 to 2,000.

The capital, Pape'ete, was founded in 1843. In 1880, France annexed Tahiti, changing the status from that of a protectorate to that of a colony. The island groups were not officially united until the establishment of the French protectorate in 1889. In the 1880s, France claimed the Tuamotu Archipelago, which formerly belonged to the Pomare Dynasty, without formally annexing it. Having declared a protectorate over Tahuata in 1842, the French regarded the entire Marquesas Islands as French.

In 1884, a fire destroyed half of Pape'ete. In 1885, France appointed a governor and established a general council, thus giving it the proper administration for a colony. The islands of Rimatara and Rurutu unsuccessfully lobbied for British protection in 1888, so in 1889 they were annexed by France.

Postage stamps were first issued in the colony in 1892. The first official name for the colony was Établissements de l'Océanie (Establishments in Oceania); in 1903 the general council was changed to an advisory council and the colony's name was changed as we have seen to Établissements Français de l'Océanie (French Establishments in Oceania). In 1940, the administration of French Polynesia recognized the Free French Forces and many Polynesians served in World War II.

In 1946, Polynesians were granted French citizenship and the islands' status was changed to an overseas territory; the islands' name was changed in 1957 to Polynésie Française (French Polynesia).

In 1962, France's early nuclear testing ground of Algeria became independent and the Moruroa atoll in the Tuamotu Archipelago was selected as the new testing site; tests were conducted underground after 1974. Over the next 30 years, 193 nuclear tests were performed in Moruroa and Fangataufa atolls. Over 130,000 people worked for the CEP, the Centre d'Experimentation du Pacifique.

In 1977, French Polynesia was granted partial internal autonomy; in 1984, the autonomy was extended. French Polynesia became a full overseas collectivity of France in 2003.

In September 1995, France stirred up widespread protests by resuming nuclear testing at Fangataufa atoll after a three-year moratorium. The last test was on 27 January 1996. On 29 January 1996, France announced that it would accede to the Comprehensive Test Ban Treaty, and no longer test nuclear weapons. Unfortunately, at least up to now, very few tests to assess the environmental impact of all this nuclear testing have been conducted, or their results made public.

French Polynesia is basically France; it is not independent from France. The President of French Polynesia is the head of government, and of a multi-party system. The current President is Oscar Temaru, who has been in power since April 2011. His lifelong goal is independence from France. But popular opinion even in French Polynesia is still that Tahiti and the other 117 islands are too dependent on help from France, and not ready for independence.

There are many reasons for this. French Polynesia does not export much, and imports almost everything it needs. Even the few things it exports are not lucrative. For example, the price of a black Tahitian pearl is one-quarter of what it was in 2000. While tourism is a major resource, it's expensive to get to French Polynesia, and expensive to lodge and eat here. There aren't enough rich honeymooners around the world to fill all the hotels. Several hotels actually closed during the 2008 global recession.

Executive power is exercised by the government. Legislative power is vested in both the government and the Assembly of French Polynesia (the territorial assembly). The French Polynesia collectivity government has control over primary and secondary education, health, town planning, and the environment.

But, as a French overseas collectivity, the local government has no competence in justice, university education, security and defense. Services in these areas are directly provided and administered by the Government of France, including the Gendarmerie (which also polices rural and border areas in European France), and French military forces. The highest representative of the State in the territory is the High Commissioner of the Republic in French Polynesia (Haut commissaire de la République).

French Polynesia sends three deputies to the French National Assembly, and two senators to the French Senate. French Polynesians vote in the French presidential elections. In the 2007 French presidential election, 75% of French Polynesians voted in favor of Nicolas Sarkozy, who was against French Polynesia independence, expressing their will to remain in the French Republic.

Total population as of the August 2012 census was 268,270 inhabitants. At the 2012 census, 68.5% of the population of French

Polynesia lived on the island of Tahiti alone. The urban area of Pape'ete, the capital city, has 133,627 inhabitants (2012 census).

At the 2007 census, 87.3% of people living in French Polynesia were born in French Polynesia, 9.3% were born in metropolitan France, 1.4% were born in overseas France outside of French Polynesia, and 2.0% were born in foreign countries. As of the 1988 census, the last census which asked questions regarding ethnicity, 66.5% of people were ethnically unmixed Polynesians; 7.1% were ethnically mixed Polynesians; 11.9% were Europeans (mostly French); 9.3% were people of mixed French and Polynesian descent, the so-called Demis (literally meaning "Half"); and 4.7% were East Asians (mainly Chinese).

French is the only official language of French Polynesia. The law states that "French is the official language, Tahitian and other Polynesian languages can be used." As of the 2007 census, 68.5% of people reported that the language they spoke the most at home was French, 24.2% reported that the language they spoke the most at home was Tahitian, 2.6% reported Marquesan, 1.5% reported Tuamotuan, 1.3% reported any of the Austral languages, 1.0% reported a Chinese dialect (half of which is still Hakka), and 0.9% another language. In the last two decades, Polynesian has started to be required to be taught in school.

During the trip, I will indeed try to memorize some words in Polynesian, as I try to do in all foreign languages I come in contact to:

Good morning/Good afternoon	Iaorana
Goodbye	Nana
Yes	E
Thank you	Maururu
Thank you very much	Mauruururoa
Good	Maitai
Woman	Vahine
Man	Tane
Love	Here

Friend	Hoa
Dance	Ori
Small island	Motu
Ocean	Moana
Good luck	Manuia

Iaorana and Maururu will be the two words I'll use the most.

Later the plan is for dinner at our hotel. The Schwartz's come by, and we are accommodated in a long table for eight. Our restaurant, like our hotel in general, is very non-fancy. The Sofitel is much more upscale. The service, like we'll find out anywhere else in French Polynesia, is slow. In fact, the national slogan in these islands could be haere maru (take it slow).

Nonetheless, we have plenty of fish and food at Le Tama'a Maitai, some of us going for the more local choices, some still preferring the known usuals. The local pia (beer) is the Hinano. Everytime we'll have beer, it'll be Hinano. We soon confirm that tipping does not exist in French Polynesia, for anything.

The currency here is the CFP, or Cours de Franc Pacific, or Pacific French money. It is linked to the Euro, and currently CFP 100 is equal to about $1. So for example half of tonight's dinner, say CFP 14000, is about $140. We always split everything with the Schwartz's, who are just wonderful company. I pay the whole bill by putting it on our room; Henry insists on giving me Polynesian cash, which of course is very helpful.

We do not even read, and fall asleep probably by 9:30pm. The way I love it!

March 21, 2016

We sleep really well. Sleeping is easy in paradise. The bed is confortable. We leave the fan on – very quiet, but we turn the air conditioning off. I love sleeping feeling warm. Like my mom. I wake up and see Paola's face, sleeping comfortably, looking towards me. She has her arm wrapped over her head, bent at the elbow. Her favorite position to fall asleep in. She did not snore all night, or at least I slept so soundly that I did not hear her. She looks beautiful. As usual. She is really lanky, long, 'affusolata,' as we say in Italian. She still has the body of a pin up.

You can tell when she is in a good mood. And in retrospect I should have guessed that these were perfect conditions. Privacy. First and foremost. The curtains are closed, and while the sun is just coming up – it's 6:30am, it's all quiet. Our room is a bit warm but great temperature. We have pushed all the light cotton covers to below our feet, and are wearing only light cotton t-shirts and shorts. Paola is gorgeous when she is half naked.

She opens the bay window on our balcony. The sun is just above the horizon, dawn is over, but the rays are still tepid, not hot; all around us is quiet. Paola, to my surprise, is completely awake. She is talkative. Unusual for the morning. But this is quite an unusual place. Heavenly. She leans over the wooden rail of our balcony. The view is breathtaking, as we had noticed yesterday.

She surprises me, "Do you want to go for a swim?" She organizes two masks. As we look into the blue and light soft green colors below us, a manta ray, dark brown and flexible softly flies in the water under us, maybe four feet below the water level. I of course jump in from our dock, head first. Paola instead gently and slowly lowers herself from the metal sturdy ladder of our overwater bungalow inch-by-inch, body part by body part. In some things, we could not be more different.

The water is warm, velvety. There are so many fish!!!! Angel fish, trumpet fish, parrot fish, and many others of which I do not know the name of. Paola has never taken a swim so early in the morning. I'm delighted to be up and active already!!

It's 7:45am, and we decide to wake up the kids. I knock gently on their heavy, sea salt-scratched, wooden door. No answer. Paola insists I try again. I knock one more time, still gently. We are on vacation after all. I now hear some noises. To my surprise, Andrea answers the door! He who likes to sleep late more than anyone I know (well, his cousin Margherita is good competition in terms of sleeping late, actually).

We eat like pigs for breakfast. Andrea has about 10 croissants, chocolate pastries and brioches. A wonderful breakfast, the four of us together. This Haere Mai restaurant with all-you-can-eat breakfast almost cannot replenish the food fast enough as all four of us gulp it down.

Andrea and I have decided to go biking. So we rent two bikes from a shop about 30 yards from the entrance of our hotel. Charlotte is a beautiful French girl, with eyes of an incredible color, a super light grey and brown, and they shine. She prepares our 'vole traditionell,' or 'traditional bikes.'

There is only one road in Bora Bora. It goes all around the island. It's 32km (about 20 miles) long. Up and down the coast. It's already 9:40am when we start, as we had a long heavy unhurried breakfast. But what a wonderful ride we have. Andrea and I are both bare-chested, no hats. I have sunglasses, shorts, and sneakers with very short socks at the ankle.

The views are fantastic. The middle of the island has a green mountain. There are wonderful tropical trees and flowers all around. We see a few shacks of Polynesian natives on the left side of the road. Most homes are made of tin and sheet metal. They would never survive in Philadelphia weather.

The sun is hot already. Sometimes around the island we catch a breeze. Sometimes though there is no wind at all, and the heat burns the skin. The view on our right – the coast - is spectacular.

The water is so clear, often very shallow near the island. Then all around there are motu, full of green vegetation and narrow sandy beaches.

It's so great to be one-on-one with Andrea. I adore him. He is such a good person. Like his mother. Serious. Smart. Caring. He does not talk much, but his thoughts are always profound. He enjoys this ride. It's important to find the right venue to be with your kids.

I've been reading actually a book called 'The 5 love languages of teenagers.' Andrea's main love language is 'Quality Time.' And I'm so happy that, while I do not speak this language that well, I found a way to speak it with him today. We are bonding. Being a father is one of the most wonderful things that can happen to a man.

The island coast twists and turns. We are making progress, but we still have much to go. The Maitai is near the southern bottom of the island. We have first headed north. We have reached and passed the airport. The north side of the island is not very developed. In fact, the whole island of Bora Bora appears pretty poor to us. Such a famous place. But, thankfully, no big villas. No luxurious high-rise hotels. Not much traffic at all on this unique road.

We are now eyeing again places we have seen before, as we passed by the west coast of the island when we made the boat trip from the Bora Bora airport to the Bora Bora main port, Vaitape. I begin to recognize a building. Our legs keep on pedaling, beginning to sense we must be past half-way done. We begin to see more people around, some kids playing on the side of the road.

As we approach the port, Vaitape, we see some official buildings, a couple of banks, some simple shops. We have not stopped at all, and we have been going for well over an hour in the now scorching heat.

As we pass some storage tin places, I see two green road signs, with one saying 'Vaitape' pointing towards the left; and the other saying 'Faanui' pointing toward the left. We pass it quickly, but soon I'm yelling to Andrea that I'm stopping, and to wait for me. I take a quick selfie with these traffic signs as background, and later post them on Facebook, saying, "Lost..." I love it.

Now we know we are getting closer, as we bike up the east side of the island. It must be the last 3 km or so, I estimate. I feel like I'm dying though. We had brought no water. It's past 11am, and really really hot. We were never in the shade, and of course are wearing next to nothing. The sun has us captive.

Andrea pushes on. I'm struggling to keep up. I've been looking towards the shore, to see if I can locate the Sofitel Motu, the hotel across the lagoon from our Maitai hotel: when I see that, I'd know I'd be close. But I do not see it, damn it!! I feel I might pass out from a heat stroke.

But soon Andrea announces: "Siamo quasi arrivati!" We are almost there. I recognize the wall of the hotel. I'm elated. We did it!! It has taken us 1 hour and 40 minutes. Not bad for 32km, or about 20 miles. Quality time with our first son Andrea. Priceless.

As we get back, Henry is at our bungalow's door. He remarks about how sweaty and destroyed we are, and appears impressed at our success of rounding the whole island. As usual during the whole trip, he has worked and organized events. His love language is 'Acts of service,' for sure.

He says he talked with a few dive centers. There is a good one close to us where we could do a refresher dive at 1:30pm at Eleuthera Bora Diving Center, nearby. I feel like dying. But I love diving!! Andrea also agrees to go. So a few minutes later I go to the concierge of the hotel and call to book the dive for Andrea and me.

Back at the bungalow, I chug down some protein bars, and almonds. A light meal indeed. I slowly rehydrate. Swimming in these magical lagoon waters helps regenerate our bodies.

Later Henry, who borrowed one of our bikes, comes back stating he is not sure that Jake and he are coming, since he cannot find Jake, who apparently went for a long kayak trip with Lori, his mother. So Andrea and I wait at 1:30pm for the pick up for scuba diving, sad we won't be with them. But as the truck approaches, we see two people sitting in the back. It's Jake and Henry, they made it!!

We go for the dive. Dan from Bretagne, a region in France, is the captain. He is short with a decent size belly, friendly and nice. There is a French girl helping him. Her name unfortunately will escape me, as it's unpronounceable. There is also Belen, an Argentinian girl who will make a movie of our dive!

As we go around the island to our destination, I admire the landscape, which is just dream-like. We see a couple of churches, one with a Christian cross. Bora Bora was converted to Protestantism and their church organized by Reverend John Orsmond in 1818.

The place of our initial scuba dive in Bora Bora is called 'Grand Canyon.' I'm so excited. I love diving. All the diving I've done around the world in the last eight years has been with Andrea. I love spending time with him, and I know he loves diving just like I do.

We are to scuba without wet suits. Dan says the water is 29 degrees Celsius even down below. So I had made the decision when we left the dock not to put one on, and the others followed.

The marine life in Bora Bora is even better than I imagine. There are so many fish, of so many different colors. The corals are not as vibrant as they were for example twenty years ago in Hawaii, or in the Maldives three years ago, but still colorful sometimes. We see several, placid eagle rays. At one point, we also enjoy a spotted leopard ray fly by us. I feel so comfortable down here on the South Pacific Ocean floor!

Not bad for what was labeled a refresher dive, since Andrea and I had not dove in three years. Once again, I feel really at ease, in my element, about 20 feet below the water surface. I try as much as I can to consume little oxygen. I attempt to float, going a bit down by deflating my lungs, and taking deeper breaths of oxygen to move up when a coral is in the way.

Occasionally, Dan asks us about our individual oxygen level. We started at 200 bars. Putting open palms at 90-degree angle to each other means 100 bars. 50 bars is when the red zone starts. I have plenty of oxygen left when after 45 minutes of delight we have to equalize a bit at 3 meters, and then come out of this paradise.

During our trip back by boat to the dive center, the French girl spots dolphins. Dan veers the boat so we can follow them. I'm impressed the whole crew of three seems to be completely disregarding any issue with time. This is Polynesia. Nobody cares about hurrying up. Dan, Belen and the French girl seem as excited to see these dolphins as we are. And they do this same job every day! I'm impressed at their generosity and enthusiasm.

The dolphins are incredible. At first I'm like, "In the South Island of New Zealand they were closer to us and the boat." But as Dan follows them slowly we soon have a dozen or more all around us, doing flips out of the water, swimming along the boat, across the boat, on all sides. It's quite an incredible sight. We stay with the dolphins over ten delightful minutes. I have a great time.

As we get back to the Maitai Hotel, I feel I am so tired. It has been quite a wonderful day already. Full, exciting, with plenty of adventure, just as I like it. I'm glad even at my age I could do it all, still. My demeanor has not changed much at all since I was 15 years old ☺.

Henry has discovered a restaurant where one can watch the sunset. It's called Beach Burger. We arrive there at 5:30pm, after about a half-mile walk, still in bright sun. The owner, Donald, lets us in even if the restaurant is still not open. And he helps us line up chairs on the balcony. We are looking straight west at the horizon.

He tells us he is of Japanese parents, was born and lived a lot in Hawaii, then in Berkeley in the US for a bit, and two years ago he bought this property in Bora Bora. He says Hawaii is too much like New York now, all skyscrapers and commercialized. He acquired the land and building for $1.5 million, and then got a container of furniture from Home Depo – the windows - and Ikea and shipped it over from the States.

He says he is doing well. Mark Zuckerberg, Justin Bieber, and many other famous people have dined here. He is still a bit upset at the fact that Zuckerberg ordered quesadillas, which are not on the menu. Zuckenberg would not hear of it, and pretended Donald – the owner of the restaurant – would get them for him from Los Angeles. Donald comments that that too much money makes you an impossible person. Too pretentious.

In the meanwhile, a majestic sunset colors the limitless sky. Orange, light blue, dark blue, yellow, purple, and soft mixes of these colors paint the few clouds, and the sky in between. We identify a cloud, and then each of us tells what we think it pictures. Great fun, and indelible memory.

I have an excellent Blue Lagoon cocktail. I'm happy and tired, the way I love it. The tiredness of a full fun day. And for dinner I inhale a fish burger. Filling and flavorful. We also have crepes au chocolate et chantilly (whipped cream), delicious!! As we'll do throughout the trip, all eight of us, Berghella's and Schwartz's, share food from our plates with others, and sip from each other glasses. A new extended family is forming.

We are done with dinner at around 8:30pm. Meals are really slow as service takes forever. Nobody is ever rushing in Bora Bora. We walk back to our bungalow, and, by 9:30pm or so, as most nights here in French Polynesia, we are happily and tiredly asleep.

March 22, 2016

Buongiorno paradiso. I wake up at 6:15am. After over eight hours and a half of heavy sleep. The horizon over the motu across the lagoon is just beginning to get a bit orangey yellow. The water color below us in the bungalow, from the glass bottom under our coffee table, is already light blue, like if the sun is first coloring with stronger light the ocean, and then the earth above it.

I put myself in bed again, to force myself to relax and veg, which are the hardest activities for me to do. I last another 15 minutes, then even Paola gets up, and I'm free to open the bay window and look at one of my favorite things, the sun. The sun has risen already. It's now a white-yellow bright ball just above the horizon, and one cannot look straight at it such is the brightness of the light burning away from it to one's retina.

We had to wake up Andrea to make him ready for scuba diving. He announces he has not seen Pietro all night. We realize that Pietro is not in bungalow 106, the one next to ours where our sons are staying. Paola switches immediately to panic mode.

I'm a bit more relaxed knowing full well we left Pietro with his girlfriend Gabby last night, and he must be with her someplace. There seems to be absolutely no criminality on the island. Everyone is super-nice. It's too expensive to come all the way to Bora Bora just to be a criminal. Plus, the island is too small to get lost somewhere. It's really a little village.

For about 10 minutes we try to figure out where to look for Pietro. I imagine he could be lying on a beach. In an empty bungalow or abandoned shack somewhere. Or back at the Sofitel Marara in Jake and Gabby's room. By miracle though, he appears. His usual smirky smile is on his face. Relaxed. Clearly very happy. He says he was with Gabby all night on a beach. I'm so happy we found him.

The issue is that he should have let us know, left a note or something. We make sure he understands. He is tired, and crashes in bed. He must have had the best night of his young life. Bora Bora. Full moon. A girlfriend he loves. I'm very happy for him, it's impossible really to get mad at the guy; he is too charming.

Andrea and I have another all-you-can-eat breakfast. We spare nothing. We eat like pigs despite knowing we are going for two scuba dives this morning. I feel pruritus from a couple of mosquito bites, but really during the whole trip these will be the only minor bug bites I'll ever get. Nobody else will complain too much about mosquitos, but we will always spray ourselves with Paola's bug repellent before every dinner.

We go dive at 7:30am at Eleuthera Bora Diving Center. Mark is the captain today, and he is a lot of fun. There is again the French 25-year-old dive instructor with the unpronounceable name with us, and today she will guide us four. She weighs only 43kg, elle est petite. They all help us gather masks and fins, and head again for the boat.

As soon as I step on the boat, I realize that I do not have my sunglasses on me. I look in the Billabong backpack I brought with me. Not there either. I ask Mark to stop the boat; we are just taking off the anchor, and I jump off back to the dive shop. Nothing. I then go back to the truck that drove us here. No signs of my lunettes (sunglasses in French) there either.

Usual Vincenzo. I lose everything. Still now. I'm much better than when I was a teenager and lost more than a dozen watches, in addition to many other items. But I've learned to live with my shortcomings. I'm not upset at all. I can always buy back the sunglasses. I just hope Paola won't yell at me too much. And that Pietro, who is clumsy like me, will improve and also learn to cope with this shortcoming.

Mark jokes around a lot. He is hilarious. He says he used to have a six-pack shaped abdomen. In fact, he compares it to a chocolate bar, sculpted. But the problem is the sun, he says. So here in Polynesia his chocolate bar of an abdomen melted, and now, as he touches his flabby belly, he says he has nutella for a belly. I almost have tears in my eyes from laughing.

When you dive in French Polynesia, you are either diving on the outer oceanic slope of the reef that surrounds a lagoon or island, inside the lagoon or in a pass. They all have a very different character. Lagoons tend to be more placid although they can definitely have current on ingoing or outgoing tides. The diving here is usually characterized by shallow coral gardens.

The outer reef slopes typically start with a reef flat in 20 to 40 feet of water and then drop at a 30 to 60 degree slope from their tops into the depths below. At some time or another during the year, most of the external slopes of these reefs get hammered by big waves. So while the coral life is abundant and healthy, it's not the lush coral of the Caribbean but rather almost all close cropped, small branching hard corals. It's just a different look.

There is a lot of fish life on the reefs and you need to keep an eye into the blue for passing sharks and other pelagics. On an incoming tide, huge volumes of water can flow into the lagoons and bring large numbers of fish. The predators, including schools of sharks, load up at the pass entrances to feed during the incoming tide.

Both the Tahitian government and Tahitian culture protect sharks and these islands have as healthy a shark population as probably exists anywhere in the world. Shark diving – where you purposely attract sharks with bait - has been practiced in French Polynesia for decades and likely originated here; yet, there are a lot of dives where you will see loads of sharks and no bait is used. They still naturally occur in large numbers here.

We go around at least half of the island to get to our first dive. We pick up two newly weds at the St Regis, a beautiful hotel. The travelguide says this is a very exclusive resort, romantic, with 145sq meters (standard size!) bungalows!!! The glittering white hotel yacht parked on their pier is luxurious and impressive. They must both be over 65 years of age. They are from Canada. She is a bit overweight, blue eyes, and smiles all the time. He is a bit more trim. He always has a smile in his face, you can tell he is delighted, in love, they hold hands a lot. It's nice to see one can fall in love at any age.

We see some rare tiki, or statue of divine ancestors, sticking out of the lush vegetation inland. Polynesia used to be polytheistic before European sailors arrived in the late 1700's. Mark also points to a monolith, a piece of rock sticking out like a thumb, he says, from the land. He jokingly says it could also be something sticking out of a man lying down. Laughter from the boat follows.

The first dive of our day is in a spot known as Anau. We see a few huge manta rays. But really huge, as big as a Smart car. They are so big at first I think they are small submarines, robot-like, put in the water for tourist attraction. But instead they are real! Their eyes stick out of their bodies at least 8 inches. I thought I had seen rays before. But I guess I never saw real manta rays! Wow!!

The corals are greyish, and do not look very colorful. The voracious crown-of-thorn starfish – Acanthaster planci – has destroyed much of the corals. Mark at some point picks up a sea cucumber from the ocean's floor. From its belly, float 10inch-long thin tentacles, glittering white.

Mark offers us to hold the sea cucumber ourselves. It's about 6 inches wide, may be 12 long. Of course I hold it eagerly. I get a few white strands of the gut stuck on my hands. They are super-sticky. They won't go away completely for 2-3 days.

In between dives I talk with Mark, and learn much about the place, and the man. The original name of the island, he states, was Pora Pora, not Bora Bora. Mark has been in French Polynesia over 20 years. His age is hard to guess, but it could be a well-aged 50 or so. He is paying $700 for his monthly rent – nothing! Like everyone else here in Polynesia, he absolutely loves his life.

For the second dive, we venture out of the lagoon. Here in Bora Bora there is only one entrance/exit to the lagoon, on the west side. Mark says this is called a pass. There are seemingly other openings in between the many motu that encircled Bora Bora, but these are not navigable, and are called, as I said above, hoa.

The second dive has also a Polynesian name: Tapu – from tabu. The water here in the open Pacific Ocean is much darker. As we descend, there are sharks everywhere. I see so many at the beginning of the dive I have a moment of panic: if they attack, I'm circled, there is no escaping.

Most are black tipped reef sharks, anywhere from a couple of feet long, to about five feet long. Closer to the bottom of the ocean, about 20-25 feet deep here, there is also a huge lemon shark, bulkier, bigger, probably about eight feet long at least. I count seven fins on his body, apart from the fin at its end.

The amazing fact is that all these sharks seem somehow unaware of us, and swim quietly all around. We all again have a great dive. Each dive lasts about 45 minutes. Later in the day, one feels the effort. Here under the water, everything is effortless. One is completely joined in nature. I forget everything else in life. Like I wrote in my Happiness book, one reaches happiness when in flow. When I dive, I'm always in flow.

On our way back, I enjoy talking some more with our guides. I love discovering facts. My 'learner' strength never leaves me. Mark states that all motu in Bora Bora are private. Maybe the most exclusive is the one owned by the Four Season Hotel, apparently the most expensive premise on the island. We pass right in front of its large bungalows, on the north-east side of Bora Bora. Some seems to have several rooms, balconies, even private little pools! They call this hotel 'the fortress.' While all other hotels welcome non-residents on their premises, assuming they'll have dinner or buy something there, the Four Season only allows its own clients.

Mark tells me on the way back that the Chinese control much of the economy of Bora Bora. The first Chinese in Tahiti were 329 Coolies from the Hakka region of China. They arrived in 1865 to work on the Atimaono cotton plantation in Papara. But the plantation failed, so the Chinese began to work in Pape'ete as merchants, butchers, carpenters, tailors and restaurant and bar keepers.

Mark tells us that five Chinese families control the whole economy in Bora Bora. One family controls real estate, one the food business, etc. They work hard, and they deserve it, is Mark attitude. It's exactly the same thing I've seen in so many parts of the world, first in South-East Asia, but also in America, and Europe, and recently New Zealand in Oceania. Today the Chinese make up an estimated 12% (34,775) of the 289,794 (about 2014 estimate) inhabitants of French Polynesia.

We pass by the former Bora Bora Club Med. When I was younger, I dreamed of visiting this Club Med so many times. I remember it was often on the front page of Club Med brochures we used to get at home, since we often go to Club Med. It has been closed for about eight years, since 2008. That was the worst year of the recession which hit Europe, and Polynesia is French, so European in economy. The Club Med site is now owned by an Australian millionaire. It used to be the life of the island, the place with some young activity. It's now an empty shell. Such a waste!

We make it back to the dive shop and land. The Polynesian lady who runs the dive center gives me several mangos as a gift. So nice, and so appreciated! I'll later give one as a gift to Lori. And I'll eat one once in the bungalow. Delicious, ripe, bright orange inside. By the way, no sign of my sunglasses, unfortunately.

We come back at 12:50pm! A long day on the water, and under the water. We find Lori and Paola in our bungalow 105. They had gone earlier together to Matira Beach, which is the most famous beach here in Bora Bora, being a large, sandy public beach. It's actually walking distance, maybe 10 minutes, from our hotel. As the travelguide said, the sand is white, and the water turquoise, so clean and brilliant one thinks it's too good to be true. They clearly also had an excellent morning.

Pietro and Gabby are still sleeping, and decline coming with us. As planned, Jake and Henry come back soon, and at around 2pm we six – including Jake Henry Lori Andrea Paola and me - head over to lunch at the Lucky House restaurant. It's only about a 7 minute walk to the left of our hotel under one of the strongest suns I've ever experienced. I'm so happy Lori – in particular - Henry and Paola are so organized, and will always find the best spots to eat at during the whole trip.

Of course seating is outside, like pretty much it'll always be until the very last day in Polynesia. We are under shade, but it is still pretty warm. I order a Salad Bora Bora, with fish. Andrea Henry and Jake order pizza. I'm more than happy with my dish, but, as I try the pizza, I discover it's great!!!

Thin crust, made of wheat which is different, more yellow than ours. Andrea had one with salami-like meats, excellent. But Henry's pizza is unbelievable; he ordered a chorizo pizza, with vegetables and an egg in the middle. Wonderful. I also try some of Jake's. He ordered a Pizza Special, pronounced with a French flair, with the accent on the last syllable. Amazing!

I cannot help myself, so I get pieces from each of them. Then I go back to the French waiter, and order one more Pizza Special. Andrea also orders a second of his pizzas. We (or at least I for sure) eat like pigs, despite the 100 degree plus temperature. I figure we certainly have burned plenty of calories. And this is indeed, no exaggeration, one of the best pizzas I have ever had!! Here in Bora Bora, of all places!!

Once back in the room, we hang out for a while with the Schwartz's. They are delightful company, intelligent, cultured, well traveled, family-first, open-minded. Then they leave. As our room is done, I lay in bed. Paola and Andrea are on our balcony, reading in the large confortable chairs. It's about 4:30pm. I take a delightful one-hour nap. So unusual for me. But my body needs it.

Then I hang out with Paola in the bungalow, and go spend some quality time with her by walking to the grocery store, where we buy more juices. We are lucky to have this small, not air-conditioned, single store near us. It's manned by local Polynesian women, all fairly obese. We'll get here during our stay in Bora Bora also some wafers, and other food and drinks.

We head back to the bungalow, so to leave the goods and let Paola dress up a bit better for dinner. We walk over to the Sofitel

Marara, where there is wifi and I have a few minutes to check about half of the 295 emails I got since we landed in Bora Bora.

At dinner, there is a Polynesian dance show. This is the quintessential Maori (Polynesian) experience. These young girls, two thin and one not, dance four or five different songs. Many of the melodies remind me of the sound of ocean waves, of the rhythmic movements of the sea. I love this soothing music. One show dance is also quite pleasing.

Most of the other dances involve the typical hip movements of Pacific dancing. The ladies wear short and very feathery miniskirts of bright colors which they make go crazy around their hips. Some of their other garments may be made of tapa, a piece of cloth made from the inside bark of the uru tree.

The company of the Schwartz's is as usual friendly, relaxed, unpretentious. I have just a Salad avec crevettes, or shrimp salad, probably 500 calories at most, a good break from the fact that at lunch I probably inhaled 3000 calories or so ☺. Paola talks about her job. I talk a bit about mine and the emails I received.

We get to bed by 10pm, thankfully Pietro is with us too this time. Gabby and he will be good, with no more all-nighters.

March 23, 2016

Once again we wake up with the sun, at around 6:15am. It's not the sun that wakes us up, it's just that 8 hours of plentiful restful uninterrupted sleep are just perfect for our human bodies. We can take it easy this early am. The first activity for me is at 10:30am, parasailing with Jake. So for now we can enjoy a bit more of our ocean bungalow.

It's raining, the first time we experience rain here. The rain is very very thin, soft, almost noiseless. It's actually refreshing. It'll be one of the few times we see rain in French Polynesia, we are so lucky. But I guess some nights later it'll also rain. The lush tropical plants and flowers all around us could not be so fresh and healthy-looking and beautiful without frequent rain.

I jump quickly in the water. I'm trying to swim as much as possible. Water is my element. Then I shower. And write a bit. By 8am we are hungry and so Paola and I go to breakfast without waking the kids up. I eat too much as usual. Eggs and jambon, i.e. bacon. Tropical juices. Pain au chocolate. Croissants. Which I cover with a coconut jam which is absolutely supreme.

We walk back to the ocean water bungalow. Around 9:15am Paola wakes the kids up. After 9:30am, I walk to the Sofitel Marara. At 10:30am Jake and I have a parasailing event waiting for us! In the meanwhile, I park myself in the large armchairs overlooking the infinity pool and the lagoon in front of the Sofitel, and check my >200 new emails, using the wifi of this hotel and the password the Schwartz's have kindly given us.

We all walk to La Plage, the small hut and beach pier where the parasailing boat will leave from. Luckily the French couple who runs this lucrative business is very nice. Not only they take Jake and me on, but they also let Paola, Lori and Henri on the boat.

The 15 minutes up on the parasail 300 feet above crystal clear lagoon waters are calm, glorious, unforgettable. Jake and I weigh in at 80kg and 95kg, respectively, so we can be later properly balanced. It is actually pretty easy to get strapped in, and lifted off the flat back of the boat. The boat came actually from California, where apparently the best parasailing boats are made.

We are very stable up there, I'm not afraid at all. It reminds me a bit of the quietness of a ski lift, up a white snowy mountain, sitting just with someone else. Quality time. Below us, dozens of different shades of blue, turquoise, cobalt, sapphire, azure, cerulean, depending on the depth of the water. Most actually looks very light pink, given the sand under it.

We rise up to 300 feet, or about 100 meters above land. Or water, I should say. One does not feel it at all. All is beautiful, stable, I feel safe, in heaven. Amazingly, we can see, from all the way up here, fish under the water surface. The most easily spotted are dark brown eagle rays.

Jake is as mesmerized as I am. The lifelong memory is worth the $. I do not get why people would not try something like this. I wish all could afford it and do it at least once in a lifetime. I'd do it again in a second, and I'll recommend it to anyone.

The French lady in the boat is friendly, as are all those living in this paradise, no matter where they are from. She tells us that her husband, who has been driving the boat, and she moved here about eight years ago. They used to have a parasailing business in the south of France. The opportunity came to buy this business in Bora Bora, and she – unlike her husband - had no hesitation. Now they love living in French Polynesia, and have two kids.

Once back on land, we all hang out at the Sofitel. I use the infinity pool, which has a fantastic view out to the lagoon. I swim with Pietro, Gabby, and some of the others. We get a pina colada. I think of the nirvana I'm in.

These islands are right out of a picture book. First of all, you don't have to be on your honeymoon to go here but, these islands are seriously romantic if you are. French Polynesia just has that exotic feel. It is what we think the prototypical South Pacific should be: palm-tree covered islands with fine white sand and turquoise lagoons.

A note on geography again: French Polynesia is composed of 118 islands divided into five archipelagoes or island groups; four are volcanic, one is coralline. The Society Islands, one of the five archipelagos, includes Tahiti, Bora Bora and Moorea. These islands are mountainous and green, often with stunning lagoons and surrounded by outer reefs and small barrier islands called motus.

The Tuamotus, a second archipelago, are coralline atolls and include Rangiroa, Fakarava and Tikehau. They are shaped like a donut with a lagoon in the middle and usually one or more passes that run from the lagoon to the open ocean. The palm trees are taller than the tallest point on these islands. The lagoons can be 48 miles across.

The Marquesas Islands, a third archipelago, are rugged, mountainous and green, usually without lagoons or barrier reefs. This is where Paul Gauguin made his home. Tahiti, although technically it refers to a single island, is often colloquially used to indicate French Polynesia.

The Society Islands are these green covered, jagged giants with great lagoons and the Tuamotus are some of the most beautiful atolls in the world. Tahiti has a vibe all its own and the Tahitians are super friendly. What's not to like about sleeping in an overwater bungalow and diving roaring passes loaded with sharks?

I swim back in the lagoon the 700 meters or so that separate the Sofitel Hotel – the Schwartz's hotel - from the Matai Hotel, our hotel. A great swim. I alternate free style, back stroke, breast stoke, and gaze to the paradise around me. My goal is to alert Andrea, alone in his bungalow, we are all at the Sofitel.

Andrea and I then walk back to the Sofitel. We hang out together in the infinity pool. Paola Lori Henry and I play pool. We are all pretty terrible, but time is not an issue. Pietro and Gabby join in and help us finish it off. I eat a vanilla chocolate and berries ice cream the kids order for me at the tropical round large bar. Delicious!!

One of the other cultural discoveries we make here in French Polynesia is the fact that sometimes one cannot tell if a person is a girl or a boy. Here at the bar there is personnel of whom one cannot tell the gender. Mahu are males who are raised as girls. We'll see many in public places too.

Later in Tahiti's airport, one woman looks about 6 feet 4 inches tall, has coarse facial features, so one can tell after the initial surprise she cannot be a woman. Mahu were present even before Europeans arrived in French Polynesia, and are now an accepted part of normal life.

Then we go kayaking. I love the fact we can do so many activities! Jake and I in one kayak. Andrea and Paola in the other. Jake and I, despite not being perfectly coordinated, go all the way to the Sofitel Motu Island in front of us and even around it. While the waters are somewhat calm in front, in the back of the island Jake and I experience a bit more waves.

Andrea and Paola do well, but they struggle a bit more keeping the kayak in a straight line, and decide not to go around the island with us. Overall we all have a great experience. It's also a wonderful upper body work-out.

Then Paola wants to go snorkeling under the bungalows in our Maitai Hotel. I happily comply. There are so many fish under us, especially under Andrea and Pietro's bungalow, since there are rocks full of corals where hundreds of fish feed.

Andrea goes running, and I'm tempted to go with him. But I resist, knowing Paola would love me more next to her. She loves quality time. And this vacation is also for us two to be well together. And I must admit I'm a bit tired, and I could never catch up to Andrea's pace anyway.

The Schwartz's (I learn from Henry that their last name means 'black' in German) come up again with the plan for dinner. The message through Pietro - who often goes back and forth a few times between our hotels to relay messages - is to meet at around

7:40pm at their hotel, so to be picked up by a van to take us to the designated restaurant.

Lori is very elegant in a black dress. The van is modern, new, air-conditioned, perfectly on time, and all these features surprise me somewhat. This island is indeed the stuff of dreams, but it is overall still simple and wild in many ways.

The Bloody Mary is a bit of a tourist trap, as Henry says, but does a good job at not only feeding us but also entertaining us. At the entrance, there are names and pictures of dozens of celebrities who have visited. I think within myself that so many of them I do not know - thankfully -, as most are Hollywood stars or famous singers. Peace Nobel price winners, great scientists, writers, philosophers, saviors of humanity are never as famous.

The food gets presented at the entrance. It's all laid out in a big long display. The eight of us get line up against it, and are instructed on what it is, and how it will be cooked. The vast majority of the choices are fish. I love it!! Everything looks really fresh. How could it not be?

Each of us chooses an appetizer and a main course. The prices are astronomical, but one is less shocked when they are told verbally to us, then if they were written. That is probably why there is no written menu. I must admit I love being able to see beforehand what I will eat. If I ever have anything to do with a restaurant, I would choose to show the food this way, too. It's very impressive.

We then are walked to our table through a floor made of sand. The table is made of wood, and one has to sit on coconut stools. Exotic plants surround us. Yes, it is the most famous and touristy restaurant on the island, but it is great nonetheless.

I have white tuna skewers for appetizer, and white tuna for main course. Everyone has fish for both appetizer and main course, except I think for Jake, who has a humongous serving of ribs. I also have a strawberry daiquiri and the kids a virgin strawberry daiquiri.

March 24, 2016

Another day in paradise. I sleep really well. The sun is a bit higher on the horizon this morning, it must be a bit past 6:30am, maybe even 7am! The lagoon in front of our balcony is very flat. There is just a minimal breeze. Long thin scattered white flimsy clouds paint the already pale blue sky. The light from the sun is right at the level of my eyes. But the rays are not burning yet.

I myself felt a bit burned through the night. Especially shoulders and arms, in particular the dorsal aspect of my hands. Someone knocks on our door: to our surprise, Andrea is up already. It's just 7am, and he's hungry. The three of us leave Pietro sleeping and have the usual, excessive, cholesterol-filled and buttery French breakfast.

Back at the bungalow, I cannot resist a quick dive in the velvety waters off our private pier on the bungalow. I figure out that soap does not mix well with ocean water: no bubbles form, the soap bar remains solid. Secrets of physics. I'll let you guess what I was doing with a bar of soap in the lagoon waters.

The pre-arranged plan for today, as usual organized mainly by the wonderful Schwartz's, is to go to La Plage where we have rented a boat with a captain who at 9am will take us wherever we want around Bora Bora. This trip has been nothing but magnificent so far. But it's about to get even better.

As usual, the four Berghella's arrive on time, which means 5 minutes early. I have no idea which one is our boat, but Henry had hinted that Lori had rented a luxurious boat. As I look around at the pier of La Plage, there is only one beautiful boat. And on board there is a dark Polynesian who is clearly getting it ready. As I walk down the dock, alone, his eyes meet mine, and he says with a friendly smile, "This is your boat!"

Wow. The name of the boat is Champagne, and it is luxurious indeed. Under a huge veranda, there are at least 10-12 confortable well-cushioned seats all around the perimeter, a table, a lounging deck. It's a flat vessel, and inside it looks like a plush living room.

Andrea, Pietro and Paola soon arrive – I went by the beach of course, they went by the road. At first they think I have invaded someone else's boat. Alfonso reassures them they are approaching the right boat. Fashionably late as usual, but not by much - as usual too - , the Schwartz's arrive – first Lori, a couple of minutes later Henry, finally after another 3-4 minutes Jake and Gabby. I'm actually happy they too are on Polynesian time, relaxed. There is no rush to do anything!

Alfonso greets us with a Polynesian song he accompanies with his ukulele. The ukulele is a mini-guitar with four strings. It is typical of Polynesia, even if it originated truly in Hawaii. Alfonso will be one of the highlights of the trip. Friendly, disinhibited, he speaks basically his own language, a mix of English (for us), Italian (also for us), some Spanish – Tiburon for shark for example, Polynesian, and only a word or two of French sprinkled here and there. I'd say that 30% of the time it is impossible to understand what he is saying. But that's part of the fun.

He is originally from the Tuamotus – exactly from Fakarava. He is 45 years old, and has been living here in Bora Bora for the last 22 years. He lives in a green-roofed house on Matira beach, which he points proudly to. His wife lives there as well, with their two sons. The 22 year old is now in the French army, while the 15 year old is studying; unfortunately, he says, this younger son's Polynesian is not that good. Alfonso feels the Polynesian language is dying.

He loves Obama, is a democrat, likes the French but not French politics, says Bora Bora is really part of Europe, if there are problems in Europe there are problems in Bora Bora. That is why with the recession in 2008 so many hotels closed, including the first one ever in French Polynesia, the Hotel Bora Bora, as well as the Club Med, and at least three others. These are still empty decrepit shells of a glorious past.

Alfonso says Bora Bora is a female. Among the many reasons he cites for this, there is the fact that there is only one entrance to the island, the pass we took a couple of days ago to get to Tapu and the shark dive. He tells us too that Marara, the name of the Sofitel Hotel where the Schwartz's are staying, means flying fish in Polynesian, and is a local fish.

We visit three unforgettable places. At the first stop, at Toopua, near the motu where the Hilton is, in the south-east part of Bora Bora's lagoon, we see millions of beautiful fish. There are also barracuda fish, much bigger, as big as a medium size shark. We swim with them, and they remain close to the boat as Alfonso is throwing loafs of bread – in small pieces of course - and many sardines at them.

It's fantastic snorkeling, as good as any scuba dive really. The water is crystal clear, the fish are bright yellow, blue, green, striped white and black, light blue, orange, multicolor, just too beautiful to be true. I can't remember the names of the different kinds of fish. But we see, here and in general all around Polynesian waters, trumpet fish, angelfish, parrot fish, Pinocchio fish, Napoleon fish, and many others.

As usual, even on the boat, we have wonderful conversations with the Schwartz's. I learn that Lori's last name is Olson. Her great-grandparents came from Sweden. She indeed looks very Swedish, with blond hair, blue eyes, and magnificent features. She is the fifth of six kids, and was always driven. She did very well in school, and excelled clearly throughout her life.

The second stop, incredibly, tops the first. We anchor in very shallow waters way past the Motu Toopua. I'm in the rear of the boat, and as I look down I go, "Madonna!!" There are over a dozens dark shadows moving like space ships maybe a foot under the crystal clear waters. There are all stingrays!

I jump in, feet first, as the water is only about three feet deep here, now in the front of the boat. And very soon I'm surrounded by stingrays. In fact, several black tip sharks, mostly about 2-4 feet long, are also swimming nearby. Alfonso, Henry, Jake, and finally

Andrea join me. The others stay on the boat, too afraid of this close encounter. Paola and Lori join later for a short time.

And it is indeed a super-close encounter with nature. As I walk around, I feel I'm being hit gently by the wings of the stingrays. They surprise me, and startle me. I cry of joy and delight. Alfonso thought of a great surprise for us.

He has several sardines he brought with him. He is now with us in the lagoon waters and he is feeding the rays. He is surrounded by them. He teaches us to hold the sardines on the top of the stingrays, and not in front or on the bottom where the mouth is. So the animals are all over him. He gives me a sardine, and for the next 10 minutes I'm in animal heaven.

I have three, four, sometimes five stingrays all over me. I can pat their top, their wings, even their tails. The body is a bit slimy, covered with an oily material that for sure makes their placid and elegant swimming easier. The tail is full of small hard points, but they are not painful to touch.

As I hold the half a sardine near my neck and chest, the stingrays basically hug me, touching my body, as they jump on top and on the side of each other to try to get to the prized lunch. In fact, I can make them almost come out of the water at least for their front, as they arch themselves to expose their mouth, which is below the front of their bodies, trying to grab the sardine.

Just lateral to their eyes, I can see their gills, from which water comes constantly in and out. Their voracious mouths are the dangerous parts of their body, as Alfonso warns us, "Be careful with your fingers, and toes, with the rays; and also with your banana." He is funny.

Back on the boat, I discuss with Alfonso where kids are born in French Polynesia. He says in Raiatea, where there is a hospital, or in Pape'ete in Tahiti. He thinks a hospital in Bora Bora is a great idea, and badly needed. He pushes me to make an investment and open one. I can, I'm European, he says.

I start fantasizing about Andrea as surgeon for the common appendix or gallbladders, Pietro to heal all the tourist sport injuries,

Paola in the pharmacy, Henry to find the appropriate real estate, Lori to do the accounting, Jake to perhaps help manage the place and its diplomatic and political hurdles, Gabby to be the beautiful 'front' of the operation, the public relations head. Dreams are free, why not dream?

The third and final stop of our boat tour is another unforgettable experience. Alfonso takes us very close to the ocean side of the reef, through a shallow canyon - hoa - between two motu islets. The beauty is to let the current - which is strong! - over the reef from the Pacific transport our bodies gently through the canal, over beautiful young – and therefore colorful - coral.

I first go and swim even closer to the barrier reef, and see thousands of empty sea shells, glistening white inside. Then as Henry instructs me to do from the boat, I turn back, and begin to let the warm, transparent current take me with it over the corals and fish below.

The corals are often colored here, either blue, or azur, or violet, or sometimes orange. Near the coral reef, the fish are more numerous. While the fish seem to be confortable with the current, I think about them enjoying being swept away from the Pacific Ocean to the calmer, gentler, warmer lagoon waters.

We end the wonderful boat trip with Alfonso still telling us about himself, the island, history, geography, and jokes. Even now, after having spent over three hours together, I miss the meaning of some of his gestures or face movements. He lastly sings to us while playing the ukulele, making up words and inserting our names in the song.

We have had also free drinks, and lots of little snacks we had carried along. We had a magnificent time, and made more indelible memories. It's sad to step off the boat. We make sure Alfonso's French boss, a nice guy from Marseille, knows how wonderful Alfonso has been to us. His tip is well deserved.

While Henry and I go pay for this adventure, we learn a bit more about the owners of La Plage. They are a handsome French couple who has been living here for many years. Their simple house is just on the other side of the street from the marine center where they work. Their kids were born here in Polynesia.

After we get back to our bungalows and reality (it still feels like a dream, though), I take a nap. What a wonderful time I have taking these naps. I never relax. Never nap. But I'm tired after all these sea activities, and the bed is so confortable, the breeze coming through the large sliding window so suave. I can't resist, my eyelids get heavy and I give in to God Morpheus, the God of sleep (as my mother would say).

Around 4pm, Paola and I walk to the Sofitel, to try to organize afternoon and evening (dinner ☺) activities. Andrea says to text him and let him know what we are doing. For now, he wants to continue to read on the wonderful balcony of his bungalow.

At the Sofitel, I quickly organize a run with Jake. I text Andrea by three means – regular text message, WhatsApp, and Facebook Messenger, just to make sure - that I'm coming back to get him and my running shoes, so to go together for a run up a steep hill he discovered yesterday. The earlier plan for a possible hike all together goes array: not enough interest, the hike is also far away and difficult to find.

So I walk back again along the shore to the Maitai, our hotel. To my dismay Andrea is no more in his room. I put on a pair of shorts, my red running shoes, and that's it. I start running, and join Jake at the Sofitel. A few yards past his hotel, we do spot the paved uneven country road that goes up a steep hill.

We go running up the hill an amazing five times. Of course Jake sprints up. I jog slowly but steadily. Even after just the first run uphill, we are sweating like crazy. I hope at some point to see Andrea join us, but no sign of him. The view from the top is beautiful, mostly with the bungalows of the Sofitel below us, as well as some local houses along the shore. The weather is beautiful, still hot and a bit humid, the sun is still shining vey bright.

We walk back eventually to the Sofitel. I'm sweating still so much that I joke with a lady at the bar that it's raining a lot close to the hotel. She first believes me, then she starts laughing hard finally getting it. I give a white flower to Lori, and a smaller orange one to Paola; I had picked them up on top of the hill, in fact they had already fallen and were on the grass, as I did not want to even disturb a flower in this paradise.

I take an outside shower on the beach. It's wonderful, with a large head and fresh but not too cold water, just right. Then I laid down in one of the beach lounge chairs and relax next to Lori, reading my new 125 emails. Andrea eventually shows up. He had had no intention of running, as he had done it the evening before. I convince him to go back to the Maitai by swimming in the lagoon. To my delight, he accepts. It has cooled off now, it's 6pm. The most beautiful part of the day, as my father says, as the sunset has slowly started.

As we swim peacefully together, Andrea tells me he is a bit worried about college at Brown, in Providence, Rhode Island, where he is going in just a few months, in the fall of 2016. He wants to do well enough to get into Medical School. And he is even dreaming of getting in UCSF now. His girlfriend Alice got in Berkeley today, and he thinks she might end up in California eventually, at least for part of her training – even if she also got into Princeton. At one point Andrea also wants to live in California. I love our time together. He is the best son a father could dream of. A priceless quality-time event, again.

This time there is not much of a break until the 7:20pm appointment with the Schwartz's, at the restaurant near our bungalows. Tonight they actually beat us there. We then walk out of our premises, to the left of the hotel, therefore more south, towards the designated restaurant for tonight, the Matira Beach Restaurant. Jake had heard this place recommended by Alfonso, our captain of the Champagne boat we cruised with around Bora Bora earlier in the day.

The food is actually fantastic. Delicious local seafood. I have an incredibly-good raw fish in coconut sauce appetizer. It's the most popular local food, called here 'poisson cru,' 'raw fish' in

French. My main course is mahi-mahi, also a local fish, in a vanilla light sauce. It melts in my mouth. The others also have seafood. I'm impressed Paola has had so much seafood this trip. She does appreciate good food, even if fish.

March 25, 2016

We wake up again by about 6:30am. Paola is in a good mood. It's the last time we have slept in this dreamy bungalow. As usual for our stay in Bora Bora, I shake the night fog one has when just awakening by getting a swim in these warm waters. As soon as I dive in, my body feels right away regenerated, anew.

At breakfast, I first have a couple of super-soft really mature kiwis and melt-in-your-mouth ripe honeydew melon slices, all sprayed with strawberry liquid yogurt. Delicious. But the healthy side quickly is over, and the fat part of breakfast starts. I devour five pastries, including 2 croissants, 2 pain-au-chocolate, and a brioche. Butter now swims in my veins, and my glucose level skyrockets. I also have a couple of glasses of a mix of orange and mango juices; heavenly.

Back in our bungalow, I finish packing my bag, which I did mostly the evening before. Then I write a bit. At 8:45am, I hear a strange noise in the quietness of the bungalow. It is the phone ringing; even this sound is soft in Polynesia. The front desk is alerting us that they are sending a porter to get our luggage. In the next few minutes we gather everything, five carry-ons and three backpacks as we had at the beginning.

On the bus which takes us and probably another 30 French tourists who stayed at the Maitai to the harbor, I'm overwhelmed by a feeling which is very unusual for me. I'm really really sad, I do not want to leave Bora Bora. This is truly heaven on earth, at least for weather, landscape, waters, views.

I grab the metal bar in front of my bus seat, and I tell Paola I'm not going to let go. They have to pry me out of this paradise. We take again the big white catamaran named Bora Bora which serves as shuttle from the Vaitape seaport to the Bora Bora airport. I take a few videos, 360 degrees around. We take a few family photos. I hope to memorize in my head these beautiful images.

The airport is so small. So tropical. So beautiful. We check in. Despite only wearing a polo, Bermuda shorts and flip flops, I'm sweating profusely, as are the others. While we wait for our plane, which is a few minutes late arriving, Pietro wants to read some of these pages from my Mac Book Air. It makes me happy to see Gabby and him interested, and approving of the draft I wrote so far. Of course, they correct a lot of the English.

Now we are flying to Moorea! Will it be as unforgettable as Bora Bora? What adventures await us? What extreme sports will I be able to practice? The travelguides say this is another paradise. Moorea means 'yellow lizard.' The name may come from either one of the island's old ruling families, or from an image a high priest saw when in Moorea. Known as the Magical Island, Moorea is one of the most inspiring destinations in the world, people say. Moorea soars magically out of the ocean in an explosion of green velvet - what you would imagine a South Seas island to be.

We get picked up by a grey van at the airport. The driver is from Moorea, he says is name is Fernando. When I inquire why so many Polynesians have Spanish names (we had met Alfonso on the boat tour in Bora Bora), he says is real name is Monumatuaho or something long and complicated like that. So he uses Fernando at work ☺. How foolish we tourists can be.

The resort we are going to is right around the corner from the airport, probably less than half a kilometer. The Sofitel Moorea Ia Ora Beach Resort is a very upscale resort. One can tell even from the entrance. It is located on the largest white sand beach of the island, called Teavaro beach, and overlooks the crystal clear lagoon waters. Ia ora is Tahitian for 'greetings,' and as a great tribute to the Polynesian sense of welcoming, so is the name of our hotel.

We get to the resort around 1:00pm or so. The rooms are not ready. We are offered fresh pineapple juice, towels to clean our hands, and lots of forms to sign, for credit card and other information. The staff is courteous.

I push our group to walk a bit around the resort to check it out, but also to have lunch. I have an ocean pizza, not worth the $27. We have a great conversation at lunch, as usual. We are becoming close friends. As Andrea and Pietro have eaten so much more than Jake and Paola during this trip, I'm able to convince the Schwartz's to treat them for lunch. They have very little anyway.

We get the rooms. Sofitel Moorea Ia Ora was one of the first on the island, since 1996, to offer the experience of staying above the turquoise lagoon. Here too we have booked two overwater bungalows. The Superior Overwater Bungalows Rooms at Sofitel Moorea Ia Ora create a soothing retreat, above the turquoise waters.

Ours is elegant, spacious, with a modern upscale bathroom and my favorite items at hotels, white bathrobes. Like at the Maitai in Bora Bora, in the main room of our bungalows there is a glass floor from where one can see the lagoon and the many fish swim happily below.

The bedroom interiors are a tribute to the islands as viewed by the French painter Paul Gauguin. The French decorator Isabelle Maffre used bright colors and soft textures to counterbalance the turquoise and crystal clear blue of the lagoon below. There is a private terrace, with chairs and a couch, as well as an outdoor shower. One can dive from it directly in the lagoon.

We explore the Sofitel. The infinity pool is to die for. It looks towards Tahiti, straight in front of us. The bar is elegant. The restaurant large. The beach white and long. I stop back at the Aquatic center. Here almost everything is for rent, from the surfboards, to the kayaks, to bikes, etc. The volleyball court I learn is for free. Diving is available, $80 for one dive, $140 for two. I'll inform Henry of these prices later.

We come up with the plan for the remainder of the afternoon. Andrea has on his training schedule 90 to 120 minutes of biking. There is no gym, so the only option is renting bikes and pedaling around the island. Somehow, I seemed to remember that the island's perimeter is 18km. The other day Andrea and I did 32km to circle around Bora Bora, so this should be easier.

I get Andrea ready, and also text Jake, who wanted to come biking already in Bora Bora. By a few minutes before 4pm, I have them all ready, on the bikes. Here we go!! It's raining a bit, which makes it even more fun. The first part, just out of the hotel, turning right and north, is a long uphill. Then we go downhill towards the Airport.

Andrea bikes fastest up front, I usually follow right behind, while Jake can keep up but with a bit of effort. He acknowledges that he has not biked at all in the last two years or so. But he likes it, clearly, is determined, and always throughout the ride gives his very best.

The scenery is fantastic. Moorea seems to be a bit more developed than Bora Bora. That is a bit surprising to me, given how famous Bora Bora is. But here and there we see houses made of cement. A few shops. Lots of amazing clear waters to our right, and jungle on our left.

The bikes are really good, much better than the ones we had rented in Bora Bora. They are relatively light, even if they are mountain bikes, and they have great gears; mine has 21 different gears, which all work very well.

I remember after about 3km to turn on my RunKeeper app on the iPhone. I use its bicycle function for the first time. About 30 minutes into the ride, it starts to rain hard. The rain is warm, very thin, but comes down in buckets. Soon the asphalted roads have huge paddles. We plane biking over them, spraying each other behind and on the sides.

Through the rain, Andrea and Jake are fantastic. No complaining, just hard pedaling. We do talk along the way some, mostly about the rain, how far we have gone, the few restaurants we pass as possible places to go with the others, and notice some Polynesian families fishing.

We are on the north side of the island, and I see we are now going through the first gulf of this coast. It's called Cook's Bay, from James Cook, the great explorer. It's really long. We go up and down the coast through small hills and valleys. The weather has improved a bit, after a long period of tropical rain. It begins to look likely that my prediction of 18km around the island is completely wrong.

In fact, as I voice my concern, Andrea says he heard at the Aquatic shop where we got the bikes that the perimeter of Moorea is actually 64km! Or about 40 miles. I see a couple of young hitchhikers along the road, and ask how far the airport ahead of us is. The male hitchhiker looks at me a bit incredulous, and says the airport is about 15km *behind* us. If we go straight, he says, it's too far, very far.

We have been pedaling almost an hour, and my RunKeeper says we have done just about 13km. Added to the 3 of so I missed since I started RunKeeper late, it makes sense we have been on the road for a bit over 16km. I decide to get the phone out of the protective plastic I had borrowed, and see if my GPS function is working. To see exactly where we are on the island, and how far we have to go.

The GPS does confirm that we are indeed still on the north side, about to enter the second major gulf. Rough eyeball estimate is that we have done maybe one third of the circle around Moorea. The sun is still high, but it is already 5pm. We have been riding for a bit over an hour. To go around the whole island we would need at least two more hours, and we would end up riding in the dark the last part, as sunset is about 6:15pm.

I'm sane, and decide to turn around. Andrea decides to continue for another ten minutes, but I feel strongly the responsibility for Jake, who is already giving a great effort. He agrees to turn back with me. I'm thankful.

On our way back, looking at the beautiful scenery inland on our right side, Jake points to long thin waterfalls coming down the side of the mountains. Like I saw in New Zealand. All is so beautiful. The sun which was shining through the rain now is a bit more gentle even if everything is drying up fast.

We have a great ride back, and end up completing over two hours straight on the bikes. My estimate based on the RunKeeper is that Jake and I did about 30km.

Andrea arrives at the Sofitel bike shop about 30 seconds after we arrive. I can relax now. An ambulance had gone by us earlier on the way back, and I had feared he had been hit by a car or something. Andrea instead tells us where he went, which is to the bottom of the second gulf on the north coast, and I estimate he did at least 34km. Great success. The dream now is to go all around the island maybe next time.

I go back to our bungalow, and take a refreshing shower. Then I relax a bit, as the bike effort has been significant. In better clothes, we head over to dinner, tonight at our hotel. Henry and Lori discover that the main restaurant has an $87 per-person buffet as the only option. We are too tired, and it is too late, to organize something outside the resort. Thankfully we are able to convince the nice Polynesians waitresses to gather three tables together near the bar, and have the a-la-carte menu instead.

We have a simple but filling dinner, all eight together as usual. I order a huge burger, but share about a quarter with Pietro, while finishing myself all the greasy fries. The $10 banana split Jake and I each order is the best dessert we have had so far, abundant and delicious, and the best bargain at the Sofitel, by far.

We talk tonight about books we have read, and compare genres and interests. And also about brothers and sisters, and grandparents – unfortunately all four parents of Henry and Lori are deceased, but it is evident they have a presence in the heart of all members of their family.

March 26, 2016

We wake up a bit later than usual, at around 7am. The beds are confortable, all is quiet and peaceful. Opening the sliding floor-to-ceiling glass doors to my right reveals a light blue lagoon, tropical paradise. Paola and I get ready for breakfast. I call Andrea with the inter-bungalow phone, to make sure he is up.

We pick him up at his place. We are in bungalow 209, then there is 207, and then his and Pietro's, 205. At breakfast Henry joins us five minutes after we arrive. While Paola is complaining that everything for breakfast was better in Bora Bora, Andrea and I are actually pretty ecstatic with the many choices. It's a sumptuous buffet.

Henry orders extra croissants and pain-au-chocolate so Paola is happy. Even if we are due to dive in a few minutes, I eat a lot, croissants, a bit of coconut cake, a chocolate soft brownie, lots of papaya, sweet honey dew, several glasses of juices, often mixing banana with orange, mango with papaya, pineapple with mango. Jake shows up on time, even with a few minutes to devour all he can get his hands on for breakfast. Great kid.

They are waiting for us at the Ia Ora Dive shop. Patrice is the dive master. We get the gear ready, and off we go. A French couple joins us. So we are six divers plus Patrice on the boat. The dive site is just about 15 minutes south of the Sofitel, on the east coast of Moorea. It's called Vaiare Pass (or Vaiare Droit, as Patrice says in French), and it's just outside the barrier reef, through a pass, on the right ('droit' in French) of the town of Vaiare. The water here is still very clear, just a darker blue since it's deeper.

As Patrice docks the boat on a white buoy, we all are looking at the many black tip sharks that can be seen swimming all around us. There are several, just only 3-4 feet below the water surface, easily visible in all their glorious, slow, wavy movements.

After less than a minute of general instructions, off we go again with our scuba diving gear in our South Pacific beloved waters. Even from the water surface, looking down just with our masks, we see already a lemon shark. As Patrice had told us, it swims slowly and peacefully at the bottom.

As we deflate our vests and descend, the lemon shark is even closer. The first five minutes of the dive, we just rest there at the bottom, maybe 6 to 10 meters below the surface, mesmerized by this beautiful shark. During the dive, I'll come to no more than a meter, maybe three feet, from the mouth of this shark. Even if I've been told several times these sharks are shy and do not attack, I get scared when one comes directly towards me, its white eyes looking seemingly in my direction. It turns away only at the last moment.

We see again so many different types of fish. So many colors. It's a great dive. We stay down over 45 minutes. Only Henry has to get out a bit early. He and Jake will call this our best dive, as we saw so much marine life, and here the corals were a bit better, even if not Caribbean-like.

Thanks to Jake, we discover we can have a second breakfast back at the Sofitel's main restaurant. The friendly staff certainly recognizes us, but lets us sit down again and scarf down a lot more food for free. I myself have also a large omelet which the friendly chef, Heinz, prepares.

After this second large breakfast, and the great dive, we are all very happy. Andrea goes for a run along the hotel white beach. Paola and Lori walk in the shallow lagoon against the current, and I join them for a bit. Then Jake and I play some waterpolo in the warm water.

Andrea has come back, and suddenly I see him going for a swim. I shout his name a couple of times as I want to join him. He does not hear me, so I dive in and follow him. As we leave the shallow waters near the shore, the current picks up, and soon becomes very strong. I only go out to about 100 yards past the last bungalow, and I'm already closer to the reef than to the shore.

Andrea goes almost another half a kilometer past me, with the current. While I wait for him in high waters, I hope to convince him to swim to the reef with me. He finally turns back and starts swimming in my direction. He is a great swimmer, but I can tell he is fighting against the current. I myself struggle a bit just to keep in about the same spot.

As he comes by me, I yell if he wants to go to the reef together. But half-heartedly. It would be very tough with this strong current. He does not even acknowledge the craziness of his dad, and swims on, strongly. I quickly decide to follow him.

My swim back is quite tough, against the current. The sea seems calm, but I find that ten hard freestyle strokes only move me a yard or so. I see Andrea getting quickly much closer to shore, and then out. It takes me another 20 minutes or so to swim back ashore, with great upper body exertion.

Later I'll find out Andrea had scraped his skin against corals during his swim, and is now bleeding. I understand now even more why he did not acknowledge me much in the water. After the blood washes off, and he dries, the coral damage appears to be mostly superficial.

I can't believe it's just still 12 noon. I'm a bit tired. I retire to bungalow 209, Andrea to bungalow 205. I get an hour nap. Incredible. I could never sleep during the day. When I get up, I have about 12 chocolate-covered coffee beans, and I feel great again.

We try to organize a boat tour for the next day, but there are not great options, and not that much enthusiasm. Then we decide we'll go for a hike tomorrow. The Lonely Plant Travel Guide says that there is a 'reasonable easy' trail from Vaiare - which is relatively close to us - to Pao Pao, lasting just two hours, so we all agree to do it together.

Once this democratic group decision is made, and tentative plans for dinner started, Jake and I go for a Tahitian canoe ride. It's quite fun, and one of the few free things offered at the Sofitel. We row past the Sofitel property, as the beach becomes public and full of happy Polynesian families. From a public place, Polynesian music is blasting. All are smiling.

In fact, va'a (Tahitian canoe) racing is the national sport, still. During our stay, in all islands, we see these canoes with attached a balancing second catamaran-like parallel hull. These outrigger canoes sometimes are single, but mostly they are made for six rowers.

On our way back, Jake and I are close to capsizing a couple of times, but manage to keep the Tahitian canoe straight up on the water. We head closer toward the reef, which we notice starts much before where the ocean waves break, and is made of beautiful orange, yellow, and mostly green and yellow corals, which come up from the sea bed almost all the way to the water edge, scarily close to the hull of our flimsy wooden canoe.

Nobody is up for volleyball. Lori, Henry and Paola are reading. It looks they are in a book club, or a public library. So I'm about to sit down finally and perhaps write some more. But Lori and Paola decide to go snorkeling. Paola and I go to our bungalows, put on masks, and swim from our ocean water bungalow 205 to Lori and Henry's ocean water bungalow 111.

There is still a pretty good current, as we experienced already swimming, and then canoeing, earlier in the day. The fish are great. There is actually beautiful coral all around our bungalows. Some is orange, bushy, thin and somewhat fragile. Some is purple and brainy. Some is blue, some is greenish, some is brownish. All is beautiful. We see trumpet fish, parrotfish, cucumber fish, fish which are yellow, blue, dark, brown, light blue. Many are multicolor.

We have red wine on the Schwartz's balcony, overlooking this beautiful, transparent lagoon. Very civilized. Henry and Lori with a bit of help from Paola have organized the restaurant; the appointment is at 6:50pm at the reception. So I jump from their balcony to the lagoon below. I had already done it from our balcony. There the bottom was only about 3.5 feet from the water level. Here I can tell it's a little deeper, and in fact it ends up being almost 5 feet, plenty confortable for a 10 feet jump from the railing. Lori and Henry are appalled. But I'm just being me.

Back at our bungalow, I take an outside rustic shower. Paola takes an inside warm educated shower. Life is good. I'm happy. All is going so well. What a marvelous day, once again.

We are actually very punctual at 6:50pm in the lobby, with the four kids getting there first!! The ride is also on time, and it only takes about 10 minutes to the Mahogany restaurant.

Once again, food is superb. This time we learn that the chef is French, his wife Polynesian. My lagoon fish soup is wonderful. Maybe the best dish I've had so far – except perhaps for the pizza! My local seabass is flavorful and well cooked, with the usual coconut cream. Even the chocolate and vanilla profiterole is great. Paola once again, like during the whole trip, has fish, a mahi-mahi. We even have some rose' wine.

The conversation tonight is on history, World Wars, grandparents and great grandparents at war, Mussolini, Napoleon, etc. Jake and Andrea participate actively, Gabrielle and Pietro listen carefully. It is a wonderful family night. By the time we get back at around 10pm, we are all pretty tired.

We all gaze at the incredible night sky. The moon is a bit less full. Interestingly, its left side is darkening; a full moon in the northern hemisphere would instead start darkening from its right side. The kids are, I hope, a bit interested if not mesmerized.

As I walk back to our place with Paola, I finally find the Southern Cross!! It's above and behind our row of bungalows, towards the west, as I guestimate. I had forgotten that the lower star is called Alpha, then going clockwise, Beta, Gamma, Delta, and Epsilon.

Getting in our spacious air-conditioned room is heavenly. It's a bit anticlimactic to call Italy with Happy Easter wishes for my parents, and then for Paola's parents. Here it's night, warm, tropical. There is morning, spring.

March 27, 2016

I wake up a few minutes before 7am. I'm a bit itchy, a lot of sun on my skin. I step out of our front door: the sun is already very bright, up well above the horizon. The resort is super quiet. Only the chirps of the island birds, and the movement of the water against the far-off coral reefs, gently fill the air.

On my iPhone, more Easter wishes, from the US, and from Italy. All relatives and close friends seem to be doing well. This is definitely a different kind of 'Pasqua' (Easter in Italian) for us. We go to breakfast at around 8am, as planned. Today's morning activity is a hike, as desired in particular by Jake.

We have read in our travelguide that there is a hike from Vaitape to Pao Pao which takes about two hours, across the hills from the south-east coast to the north coast. It should be doable. At breakfast, we eat way more than we should for a group of inexperienced hikers. I once again have fruit, yogurt, plenty of croissants, nutella, juices, etc. Probably at least 2000 calories. Paola and I even make several sandwiches for lunch, about seven, and we sneak them out, me as usual in my hat, Paola in her big white elegant purse.

Unlike other events, we have not planned this one in detail, and we have not booked anything. So I go with Henry to the check-in and concierge desks to try to organize it a bit better. Henry would like us to get a guide, someone to lead our trek, take us to a nice one, and make sure we get back.

The lady at the check-in desk begins to get on the phone. From the best, newest and most comprehensive brochure of Moorea they have, she starts dialing number after number. There are about six hike tours listed, and she calls them all. But without any luck. They are booked, or off for Easter, or it's a bit too late to call the same day. We are past 9am already.

The agreement at breakfast had been that we were supposed to all meet by the check-in desk by about 10 minutes past 9am, but many stroll in a bit late. It does not matter anyway; the hike begins to look less likely. In the meanwhile, the sun is getting hotter and hotter.

I ask the lady at the check-in desk, a kind Polynesian girl about 30 years old, with the usual pregnant-looking belly of this part of the world, to then please call us a couple of cabs, or a van for eight, or some means of transportation to get to the trail in Vaitape, about 3km (2 miles) away.

In the meanwhile, the line behind me at the check-in counter has gotten bigger. There are at least 3-4 other families in line, and the other check-in desk personnel is busy. But my check-in girl is an angel, and calls about five or six taxi and/or van places. I'm hopeful she must be able to find someone. The list of taxis she has is long. We are at the Sofitel after all. I plan to then ask the taxi driver for advice on where to find the trail, since we have no idea of where exactly it is.

But no luck. She cannot find us any transportation. While she is dialing now, she starts servicing some of the people in line, as I have shyly moved to the side, feeling sorry to let the people in line wait so long. She keeps on smiling to me, and I can tell from her eyes she is imploring me to give up, as clearly she cannot find anyone.

I understand. I take the brochure myself, and start dialing with my own iPhone all the local taxi numbers listed, especially the ones in Maharepa, a small town nearby. I call all of them. I get either no answer, or "I'm occupied," or "We do not work today." I'm not mad, I completely understand, it's Easter.

It's time for a family meeting. By now they are all standing at the entrance of the check-in area. I give the grim update. No tour guide. No taxi. No transportation. The options are bagging the hike, or start walking ourselves. Henry has been voicing that option for a while. He even tried to just find out about just taking a walk around the hotel, but we find out there is nowhere else to go near the hotel on the road that goes along the perimeter of the island.

So we get on the road ourselves. It's late, about 9:30am, we took it easy I guess a bit too long, and it's hot already. We know there are about three kilometers to Vaitape and the start of the trail. As we get to the hotel car entrance of the Sofitel, we turn left (instead of right like when we went biking). We are already in unfamiliar territory.

It's scorching. I'm sweating profusely. I'm wearing a beach white long-sleeved shirt, a swimming trunk suit, and my best running shoes. This great apparel will probably contribute to save my life later in the day. All eight of us are walking, at different paces, and switching subgroups as we go along, on the narrow grassy shore side of the road.

I walk mostly ahead of the pack with Lori, who is clearly in shape and a fast walker. On our right side, the asphalt of the main road. On our left, houses along the shore. These are in general not mansions, but certainly better looking and more modern and beautiful than the shacks which mostly made up the housing in Bora Bora.

Miraculously, despite the strong sun and the sweating, all eight of us get to Vaitape. It's about 10:30am. We are already dehydrated. We buy a few bottles of water, which we drink eagerly, leaving little left over water. Tonino, one of my two best men at our wedding, calls my cell phone with FaceTime. I love the guy. I can show off my new sunglasses and Costa Rica large brim hat, with this Polynesian island and the port where the ferries come and leave for Tahiti all around us. I have Pietro Andrea Gabby and Jake say hello to him and his wife Nicoletta. I even get to say hello to his mother Teresa.

Paola and Henry check in some detail the ferry terminal. As Lori and I had already discovered, everything in the terminal is closed, there is no way to buy the tickets we need to get back to Tahiti on Tuesday. At least we take a picture of the timetable, and find out there are Moorea-Pape'ete ferries several times a day.

Gabby and Pietro have already decided they've had enough. We have hiked for an hour, they have an hour to go back, and it's already blistering hot and sticky. I'm happy and surprised they came so far. They are so in love. They just want to be by themselves. Neither of them is that driven and determined, or adventurous, at least for now.

The other six of us, Andrea, Paola, Henry, Lori, Jake and I push on. I'm told by the locals we should cross the trail just around the next curve in the road. As we walk, I ask anyone along the road for Pao Pao. It begins to look like the fork on the right for the trail to Pao Pao is coming up.

In fact, one probably 25 year old, but 45-year-old-looking, tanned dark thin Polynesian man follows us, and keeps on pointing to the right turn we ought to take, making sure we do not get on the wrong path. He is very nice, while he does not speak a word of English or French.

Just before a corner shack of a supermarket, in front of which a few Polynesian women are chatting, we find our trail. It's a dirt trail, but it is dry for the most part, at least here at the beginning. For the next kilometer or so, it goes up towards the mountain in front of us so very slightly, on a gentle incline.

We have no hesitation that we'll walk at least a bit of it. Around us we are gifted with interesting scenery. We see a very rough soccer field, with rusted goals and no nets. Andrea and I get excited. True non-French speaking Polynesians live here, a bit inland. To each of them, I ask, pointing to the road ahead, "Pao Pao?" When they shake their heads up and down, I then say, "Maururu'," thank you in Polynesian, and receive then back a big smile. Andrea and Jake make fun of me as I continue to do this throughout our initial Vaitape-Pao Pao trek.

The houses are simple, mostly on the right side of the trail. We see roosters, chickens, pigs. The vegetation is lush, with beautiful plants, and flowers. We say hello to the last Polynesians we'll see for many hours. The road begins to become grass and mud a bit more, and narrows.

The vegetation is interesting, different, foreign certainly, with only a few recognizable plants. Some of the trees have red barks, like the miki miki. We do see strange fruits and flowers along the way. We have seen some of these flowers in the skirts of Polynesian dancers, and especially behind their ears. The tiare is a small white flagrant gardenia which is the symbol of French Polynesia.

As the trail begins to climb up more steeply, houses disappear, and only lush tropical forest is around us. We encounter some forks in the road. There is no signage whatsoever. We have to guess a couple of times which fork in the path to take. Henry's earlier idea of getting a guide was indeed a great idea!

In fact, after another such bifurcation, we go down a dead-end path. It is at this point that Henry says he is ready to turn back. We do not discuss it much, but it is implied that Lori, Andrea, Jake and I are ready to take the steeper alternate route up the mountain, and keep on. Paola states her right inguinal area is bothering her a bit, and so she prefers to head back with Henry. This is not the time or place to force anyone to do anything they don't want to do.

So Lori Andrea Jake and I are now going up a trail with at least a 30-40^0 incline. Pretty steep. We pass the last inhabited location - which we can't see through the vegetation, where someone - who we also can't see, must be working the terrain, as he is making some noise. We are left with wilderness only. We are soon under big trees, with roots crossing our paths. Fallen tropical flowers, fruits and nuts, the size of an oval golf ball, brown and slippery, are under our feet.

In one area, we see the last remainder of 'uncivilization.' Some big trees have been carved with names of people, lovers, etc. I'm appalled, but at least we know some people have been in this far-away place. We keep on climbing up. It's a bit dark, the vegetation above us is thick, and not much light at all comes through.

On a steep ascend, we see in front of us a blond kid, not more that 2-3 year old, bare-chested and barefooted. Nobody else is with him. He is all excited and talkative, and describes something to us quickly in French. I think I have just met Tarzan! How can this kid have even made it to here, be all alone, barefooted in the treacherous terrain? He instead seems to be in his element, is smiling, supercute, his almost white hair shines even in the dim light.

After a minute or two of trying to converse with us, once he realizes his quick childish French is mostly over our heads, he decides to keep on his descent, and so we carry on with our ascent. Thankfully, after about another minute, here comes down the mountain a man with a very young child in his arms. Tarzan's dad!! How is he walking the impossible terrain with that extra weight, impeding his balance?

A few more meters up, and a lady holding the hand of her 4-year-old daughter crosses our path. Here is Tarzan's mother! The young child is also very talkative, of course in French. The mother, in broken English, tells us her daughter would like for us to put more stones on top of a pile of rocks up the mountain. She is so cute!

We carry on. Amazingly, my cell phone rings. It's my great friend Daoud, wishing us all Happy Easter from Philadelphia. As I tell him excitedly we are in the middle of nowhere in the Polynesian jungle, he quickly says bye. He had earlier texted about some medical advice, and I'm glad I was able to help his family some.

After another five minutes we cross the last human being we'll see for the next several hours. He is a French guy, maybe in his early forties, sweaty and smiley. We ask how far we have to go up the mountain. He says, "Vingt minutes, and demi heure pour la descent." We are relieved: only 20 more minutes going up to the peak, and 30 minutes down the other side to Pao Pao, or so we assume, seems doable.

We continue with the climb. Now the going is getting tougher, as we are heading straight uphill, like climbing massive stairs. When we get to a high point that seems promising, we find there is another peak past it. It takes us at least 40 minutes to finally get to the top. Thinking back, we figure perhaps we misunderstood the guy who said 20 minutes? We hope the descent on the other side is quicker and easier.

We are on the ridge of the mountain, between Mt Mouaroa (880m) and Mt Mouaputa (1207m). There is a three feet by two feet small levelled open space where we can sit down a bit. The view from here on top is beautiful. Looking back towards Vaitape, we can see the ascent we just did, the port, the shining waters of the South Sea. We take pictures.

Ahead, on the other side, looking north-west instead of south-east, we see mostly more mountain ridges, completely covered in thick bright green vegetation. There seems to be some farmers' houses in the very far part of the valley. We drink a bit of water. We imagine the worst is over.

Now we figure the path will be all downhill, so we should be fine. As we start the descent, I realize my cell phone is out of batteries. I was using RunKeeper, receiving phone calls, taking pictures... Now we are really by ourselves, as nobody else has cellular or internet capabilities.

As we had reached the top, the narrow one-foot-wide path ended in another path, at a 90 degrees angle, going along the mountain top ridge, with the option of going right or left. We had taken the right. We had found the clearing where to rest. Then we had continued, only to find the road led nowhere. The only choice was to go back on our trail, and continue down on the path we would have taken as we would have turned left once on top.

This path begins to take us a bit downwards. We walk down the side of the mountain. It's very difficult hiking. The trees and vines are often in our way. We have to continuously duck under fallen trees. Or climb over them. The path is always on the side of the steep mountain, with roots and trees on the left side and below or in front of us, and a cliff on the right. As it has rained yesterday, and it is always humid here in the jungle, often we are walking in narrow muddy small paths.

We hike and we hike. For over an hour. Didn't the last French guy say 30 minutes for the descent? There is no signage whatsoever. Except at one point a rusted sign on the side in French, abandoned. Among the many phrases on it, one says soothing like, 'No trespassing.' We figure it must be an old sign from somewhere else. Very rarely there is a break in the vegetation around us, enough to see mostly green forest covering the mountains all around us.

Sometimes we rejoice as the path does go down. Soon to be concerned again because we are climbing up again. Clearly we continue to just go on the side of the mountain, not down. It begins to feel like we are going nowhere. We keep on looking on our right side, the side down the mountain, but there is never a sign of any trail to go downhill.

We do at some point begin to hear shots all around us. Lori and I figure it could be fire works. Or actually Polynesians shooting around at wildlife – but we see none really, only a rare bird. We keep on walking on the side of the mountains. The vegetation gets thicker and thicker. At some point, a couple of times, we have to duck and hug the side of the mountain to go under mangroves.

The terrain is getting ridiculously difficult. We feel we are in a survival adventure. Moreover, the shooting is getting closer, and more ominous. Lori I guess is getting more worried now that these are actual gun shots, or rifle shots, because, all of a sudden, in the deafening silence of the mountain, she shouts, "Attencion!" I figure she is trying not to get us shot.

We keep on going and going. Andrea is usually in front of us. Later Lori takes over. We are all following, stumbling, hoping for a way down. But none seem to be visible. We pass a beautiful area with thick bamboo trees. We have been walking now from the peak at least an hour and a half. I have been carrying the backpack the whole time. I'm getting pretty tired. I ask Andrea if he can carry it now. He bravely takes it.

As we are getting a bit disheartened, Lori spots on our right side some plastic red and white markers, rapped around tree trunks. Yeah!!! Finally some signs of life. And a possible way down. I'm happy now. The markers take us straight down the side of the mountain. Now there is no more identifiable path. But we find about 8 red-and-white plastic markers in a row wrapped around tree trunks. It's about past 2pm. About time to find a way out.

The underbrush is thick with trees, huge roots, vines that block our way, leaves, fallen tree trunks, rotten branches, green moss, tropical fruits. Finally, as we slide down, we cross what looks like a path, at 90 degrees from where we were descending. On our left, there is a nearby creek, where one would think the path would continue to.

The creek is small and has crystal clear waters jumping through rocks and vegetation. I imagine the way forward is on the other side of the creek. So I venture there, careful not to slip. I fight branches, vines, roots and trees unbelievably close to each other, but there really seems to be no way through on this side anywhere.

Somewhat defeated I turn around. I tell Lori that there is no way through on my side. She then goes and check the opposite direction, away from the creek, on its right side, where perhaps she could find the start of another trail. In the meanwhile, I, exhausted, ask Andrea, who is sitting by the creek, to give me some empty plastic water bottles.

I fill three of them, two small ones and one big one. I pour the clear water on top of my head. My white long-sleeved shirt is already completely wet from sweat. The fresh water feels great on my head, pouring down my chest first. Then I pour some more so it travels down my back, too.

I notice that in the transparent plastic bottles, the creek water is just a tiny bit darker than bottled water. A tiny bit. One could easily mistake it for pure water. The temptation to not only pour it on oneself, but also drink it, is high. Problem is, as a couple of drops have made their way through the right corner of my lips, and

I've swallowed them, I feel a bit of stomachache. My belly is otherwise empty. A warning to not drink this water.

I throw the two filled small bottles at Andrea. He is not too happy about carrying all this water. I walk over towards him, and give him the big bottle, too, full. I feel we all can use it to cool off for the rest of this hike. Especially since we still have no idea how long it will last.

Lori comes back saying there is no path forward on the opposite side of the creek, either. Where next, then? The only way possible at this point seems to be through the riverbed. Andrea seconds this idea, too. We figure we already came down the mountain a bit, and the creek is going somewhat straight down. The creek will eventually lead us to the sea, or a village, or a bigger river, or some house, some rescue.

Andrea and I forge ahead, downhill. For the next 15-20 minutes, we venture downstream. Sometimes we have to walk on the slippery waterbed rocks. Sometimes on the sides of the creek, under or through mangroves, holding on for dear life to rotten and unstable trees, or branches, or vines.

At some point though the river is no longer an option, so we veer through its right side. We are still going down, but slowly, as the jungle gets to be even more of a tangled mess. Now for quite a while we have been away from any marker, or any recognizable path. The forest is getting thicker and thicker, instead of easier.

I think back and do not understand the earlier white-and-red plastic markers: why where they there? Could have they led us nowhere? Where did we miss the right path? We have been now almost two hours past the peak. The last guy we had seen had said half an hour to get down. Lori now thinks we misunderstood. Maybe he said, "Demi jour," not "demi heure." Half a day, not half an hour. Nonetheless, at this point we seem to be going nowhere.

I try to venture next on the left side of the creek. Here too there is no path down, no way through the mangled mess of vines, trees, foliage, branches. I figure the only way to continue down has to be again through the creek bed. There is no other possible way.

We are now back on the right side of the creek. I keep a bit left, towards the continuous running noise of the water.

The creek is steeply below us. We are at least 20 feet above it now. I can see it, dark, through the trees. It's not feasible for everyone to make it down to the creek. So I announce I'm going to explore it, see if there is a way through down there.

I have to basically slide down on my backside down mud, through roots and trees. My bathing suit is getting completely brown. It'll be something to throw away if we ever make it back. I'm really doing dangerous things now. I could just crash down this steep incline to the rocks below. Or strangle myself with a vine. Or twist an ankle. Or break a bone. I hold on for dear life to some trees with my arms, way behind my body. Andrea is up far from me, but closest to me. I beg him not to try to come down.

Once I'm down closer to the creek, maybe 6-8 feet from it, I can see better the riverbed ahead. Despair sets in. The mangroves cover it completely. Even crawling like Marines down on top of the middle of the riverbed, I cannot imagine we could get through. The mangled mess of vegetation is impenetrable. I look right. Same. I look left. Blockage, complete blockage.

The worst part of this hike is now, seeing that the creek bed is blocked. I announce my findings to the rest of the crew. And I crawl myself up the steep river side hill I just came down, hurdling myself up by pulling with my arms on roots and trees. I begin to think that certainly, if there is no way forward, we should consider trying to find our way back.

Lori announces, "We should go back." I immediately concur. There is clearly no way forward. It's past 2:30pm. Even if we have to hike back 2-3 hours, at least we should make it before sunset. I'm a bit scared. We have little food, and almost no drinkable water left. And we have no idea about where we are.

Or how really to get back. While retracing our steps back is clearly the right decision, I wonder if we'll be able to find our way backwards. We are very far from the peak. If we take another wrong turn heading back, that could be the end of us. Or at least a night in the wildness. In the middle of the jungle. In a far away semi-deserted island. In a huge archipelago. In the middle of the biggest ocean, the Pacific. Oh my.

Andrea and Jake try to fight the decision to go back by retracing our steps. Andrea says it will take us at least three hours; and he is already exhausted. Jake is silent in his suffering. And concerned, as we all are.

Lori has started heading back. The ascent is very steep. We have been going through the jungle, without a path to follow, or any signs, for probably at least 30 minutes. The first goal is to find the red-and-white plastic signs on the trees, the ones that led us astray, really, in the first place.

It looks like the ascent is even more complex than the descent. We go up for a while, but nothing is recognizable. It's just a mess of trees, branches, vines. The creek this time is on our right. I can see Lori leading us up. She is now veering towards the creek, as the only possible guiding principle.

She begins to talk, breaking the silence of fear which is enveloping us. She is by a big 8-9 foot high rock, by the side of the creek. She seems to recognize it. I do too. Or maybe I'm just hoping. What if we cannot retrace our steps? There is no way anyone would ever find us here.

Lori and then the three of us boys make it around this big rock, covered in humidity and moss. On the other side, a white-and-red plastic sign around a tree! We found the first of what we hope will be a long series of spots we can recognize going back. We now also identify the small break in vegetation, the place where we had to decide if to go right or left, which eventually led us no good way down.

We have to now retrace our steps by the eight or so white-and-red plastic strips tied around trees. It is actually very steep to go again straight up the mountain. I can't believe we are still going up. I begin to dream of making it eventually back to clear lagoon waters. To the infinity pool. For now, we have not even been able to see the sun for hours.

Now the next task is to find the trail, on top of the line of the white-and-red signs. And I'm not really sure how many of these bands there have been. By miracle though, we do find the trail. I announce the sighting with a bit of joy in my voice. We could turn right and proceed further in the unknown.

But we are set on going backwards. Lori says now this trail should lead us straight to the peak of our first mountain. I'm not so convinced the road back will be so easy to find, but I trust her, and agree this is by far the best choice. If anything, we'll get closer to where we started, and our dead bodies will have a higher chance of getting found eventually.

Andrea and Jake are still not too happy about Lori's and my plan to retrace our steps back. Andrea again states it is too far for him to make it. Jake occasionally keeps on falling along the route. Lori is resolute and is leading us up the trail.

We hike back for over two hours. My knee is killing me. I've been operated twice on my left knee, once in 1989, then again in 2006, always on the left medial meniscus. In December, just three months ago, I was almost paralyzed there by arthritis, and eventually only a cortisone injection by my colleague in interventional radiology got me back walking normally.

We stop every 15-20 minutes, exhausted. We pour water from the creek on our heads. Actually Lori pours it just on her arms. I'm getting more tired, but less scared. At some point, I realize that indeed this super long trail will lead us directly to the top of the peak we reached at the beginning of our hike. The realization, and the thought that Lori is right, gives me great hope. But we are not there yet. It's about 3:30pm, and we are still very far.

Bit by bit, we find some landmarks. First a rusted sign at the bottom of a tree, which says in French something like, "Do not proceed further." We should have listened to it earlier, Lori and I comment.

Then the bamboo tree gallery. Andrea and Jake once in a while still complain. I ask for breaks as I feel at times a bit dizzy, and do not want to fall. Lori is resolute, always in front, and pushes us. She is the leader.

Jake slips at least three or four times in a major way. Andrea a couple of times states he is not going to make it. I say that from now on I'll always go to church on Easter, if this is what happens if one does not.

But we are continuing to make progress. We had known that one point to look forward to was the part where we had to crawl under mangroves. We find them, finally. Going up through them is even harder than descending through them. I slip a couple of times. The rocks I move under me roll down loudly and menacingly for tens of feet. I'm glad I'm not one of those rocks rolling down the steep mountain terrain.

Finally we get to the original peak of the mountain. This was the goal I had dreamed of almost two hours ago, when we started heading back. Now it would all be downhill. And known terrain, even if steep. At least, even if somebody broke a leg or got injured, they would find us here, probably.

We sit down on the top in the open space where we sat hours earlier. We almost finish the little water left, a tiny sip for each of us four. I have some nuts and some chocolates, warm and melted. The others also eat some, and we share a granola bar. We are relieved to be much closer to getting back to civilization, and safety.

Lori and I get up, and head down first the steep trail back to Vaitape. My legs here are really weak, as I imagine are those of my mates. My left knee hates going down so steeply, and aches. I'm afraid my arthritis will come back with a vengeance, cause me serious pain and maybe force me for the rest of the vacation on a chair.

But down we go. Slipping here and there on unstable fallen branches, or oval brown wet fruits. As we have been doing all afternoon, Lori and I call out slippery terrain, unstable pathways, anything tricky to manage along our trail. After a while, we cross the part were trees had been carved with names. I do know we are getting close now.

It still feels like it's taking forever. Such a long road. I guess I must be tired, and feel it more. The ones who are doing the best now are Jake and Andrea. They are galvanized that we are almost back to safety. They sprint ahead of me and then Lori. They want to run this last part. And a few minutes ago they almost gave up! Ah, youth!

Lori tells me we better keep up, as we do not want to be left alone. We reach more landmarks. We begin to hear some familiar noises. Andrea is delighted seeing a rooster again. We pass the place with the pigs, and we reach the first shack along the left side of our path.

There is a creek again on our left, now running more smoothly, as the terrain is starting to flatten. Even this almost level trail back is long, I forgot; it is probably a kilometer. We see Polynesians playing volleyball. My legs are killing me, but the smile on my face is getting really big.

Andrea and Jake are so far ahead we do not really see them anymore. We wonder if the shop at the corner, where the Vaitape-Pao Pao trail had started, is still open. I'll buy every liquid in it!! Lori and I now have been talking for a while, relaxed. The deafening silence on our way back, before reaching the peak of the mountain and a shot at safety, is gone.

We can see from afar that the corner store is closed. Too bad. I had told Lori at the beginning of the last straightaway, leading directly to the sea, that I would not stop. Meaning I would keep on walking straight, and jump in the sea. But the kids instead, from far ahead, signal to us with their arms that they are turning left and continuing on our way back.

But it's three more kilometers to the hotel. I'm afraid my knee will give out. I've been afraid that my collateral ligaments, or my cruciate, would break in my left knee. To Lori's request, I resist jumping in the ocean. But I'm determined on finding something to quench my thirst and dehydration first, and then a ride back second. Lori has already pledged she'd pay even $100 for a car ride back.

We do not see Andrea and Jake anymore. My guess is they are at the Shell station, where there is probably a store. Indeed, as we get near it, I see Andrea and then Jake coming out with their hands full of cold bottles of water, four of them, and a huge CocaCola bottle. I grab everything that is passed on to me, and drink, elated.

After over a liter of fluids in, I borrow some money from Lori, and go in to buy something else. Once I see ice-cream, I make that my choice. I buy two, one vanilla bar and a chocolate Magnum. Andrea refuses to get one. Lori buys one too for herself. As I walk out, I offer one of my ice-creams to Jake, who picks the chocolate Magnum. All are happy. As Lori will say later on, this is the best ice-cream we have ever tasted! I begin to think I won't die.

I see in front of us opposite the gas station a couple of yellow tour buses, and what seems to be a taxi, even if with no sign on it confirming it. Andrea himself states aloud that this type of white van with something red written on the side was some kind of taxi. As I approach it, there are two young guys with whom I cross eyes.

I ask politely in French if it's possible for them to take us to the Sofitel. One of them I realize is in charge of the taxi. He looks at his watch. He confirms with me we are all ready to go. Indeed, I turn around and Andrea Jake and Lori are within a couple of yards from me. We all look like crap. Like survivors. I must smell terrible. I have mud all over my white shirt, filthy bathing suit, and you can barely tell my sneakers were originally bright red.

But we are in luck. The kind young Frenchman says he was waiting for the ferry boat to arrive, but if we get on the van quickly he can take us. I ask how much, and he says 1,000 CPF, the equivalent of $10. Even cheap given the prices in Moorea. We get back to the Sofitel by 4:30pm, in air-conditioned heaven. Lori tips him another $10.

We are super-tired as we walk into the hotel. I can barely move my legs now. We see Paola, who is appalled at the way I look. Muddy, disheveled, destroyed. But I made it!! The kids are even more tired. Lori is stoic and unbreakable.

I go and take a very long shower. One of my toes is completely blue. I'll eventually lose this nail. This is certainly due to the pressure from my foot sliding down in the running shoe while trying to manage the impossible terrain. Then I go to the pool with Andrea. The hope I had hours earlier becomes reality. I'm in the infinity pool, with my loved ones. I stay in at least an hour, reliving with the others our adventure. Paola, then Henry, then Pietro and Gabby all join us in or near the pool.

I get bad leg cramps while in the pool. The muscles in my hamstrings, quads, calves, and feet, seem to be complaining about the 7 hour-long hike. Pietro is nice enough to get me a banana shake. Ten minutes after I glob it down, my cramps resolve. Maybe coincidence, but I'm happy the cramps won't come back anymore, even later in my sleep, as I feared.

Next activity is getting together for rum cocktails at the Schwartz's water bungalow, number 111. I water down my drink substantially. Lori even has Easter treats for us, which I grab with full hands. I'm lying on the deck, feeling a bit better with every chocolate, every sip of fluid.

We have dinner again at the Sofitel's bar, outside, under the stars. I have a club sandwich, decent not great, and the wonderful banana split. I'm so tired. We talk about different trips, as well as books. I'm glad to go to bed by 10pm, and sleep soundly, without cramps.

March 28, 2016

I wake up anew again. I write a bit. It's quiet, a bit cloudy. I love these times alone, me and my brain. When I write I withdraw into my world, my man's cave. It relaxes me tremendously. Then Paola, slowly, wakes up, and leisurely gets ready.

We have a huge breakfast as usual. Heinz at the crepes and pancake grill is sweating a lot. He jokes that he gets so thirsty sometimes that he wants to drink the crepe mix! The others arrive, all without rush. Even breakfast here is a long and unhurried meal.

I eventually get up first from the table, and move myself to the nearby hotel beach. I get eight lounge chairs in the best spot, and I'm happy I can contribute to camaraderie for our group. I notice that there are less people here today. It's the Monday after Easter. I check some emails, and then write some more.

The others are slow to come. I'm glad I did not wait and came early to this paradise. The Schwartz's must be getting their luggage ready maybe. I swim a bit to refresh. The water is so clear. It stays shallow for a while, at my belt, at least for about 30-40 yards from shore.

For the first three meters from the wet sand, the water is not even blue, it's just transparent, with a bit of yellow silver reflections from the bright sun. Then it begins to be azur, really a very light blue. 'Celeste' we would say in Italian. The colors are so beautiful. This is as good as it gets in terms of the seashore.

The others slowly arrive, and suddenly I'm so happy all eight lounge chairs are occupied by our group. I love it that the kids are with us. We play volleyball in the water. The game is called 'Schiaccia 7,' or 'Spike 7,' a game Pietro and Andrea play every day at the beach in Italy in the summer.

Basically the rules are that at the 7th touch, one can spike towards someone else. If the desired recipient gets it, the spiker gets a point. If the recipient is instead able to catch the ball, the spiker loses a point. We have a great time playing. The Schwartz's get into it!

We play for quite a while, then we are all afraid we are getting fried in the hot sun, even if we do not feel it in the water. I take a great shower together with Andrea and Paola. What a perfect day. We made the right choice to stay here at our hotel, and enjoy this paradise.

We now read a bit on the beach lounge chairs, enjoying the shade and the magnificent view. Across the blue lagoon, the outline of the bigger island of Tahiti. One by one, the Schwartz's leave us, as they have a plane to Tahiti at 4:30pm that afternoon. Sad to see them go, but we'll reunite the next day. Pietro and Gabby are in charge of organizing where we'll meet.

Paola and I later go to the concierge desk to book the restaurant for the evening. And the taxi to take us to the ferry back to Tahiti for the next day. We come back and spend some more quality time on the beach.

As Pietro comes back from saying bye to Gabby, he and I play 'tiri in porta': Pietro shoots the ball to me while I stand in knee-deep water, and play goalie. On a good shot by Pietro directed to my left, I jump to touch the ball as it zips by, and my wedding band comes flying from my extended left arm and hand. I cry for help.

Pietro is quickest to come over with a mask. I have not moved. I look under me towards my left, where I saw the gold ring flying into the water. For a minute or so I do not see anything. I beg Andrea Pietro and Paola to come over and help. A few moments later, I look a bit closer to my left foot, about 30cm from it, and I visualize my wedding band. I extend carefully my left hand in the crystal clear water, here about a meter deep, without even moving my feet, and grab firmly the ring. I got it. It's the 4th time I lose, even if for a short time today, my wedding ring.

Andrea and I later go on the Tahitian canoe. It's fun to do it with him. Unfortunately he only wants to try it for a little bit, so we are soon back on shore, but not before an excited Paola has snapped some pictures.

Paola and I then go snorkeling together under our bungalows. We see so many different kinds of fish. Small as a thumb, some bigger than a football. Yellow, white and yellow, blue and yellow, blue and orange, pink, green, red, red and yellow, orange and red (one of my favorites), sand colored, white, transparent, white orange blue and yellow, and many others. Some are all together, 10 or 20 or 100 together.

Some are more solitary. Occasionally two of them are swimming very fast after each other: I wonder if it's love or a fight. Or maybe both. Some are long and thin, some are small and oval, some are more round, some are very flat and upright; trumpet fish are long and thin as a long straw. Incredible variety.

There is coral all around us, and the fish come in and out of it, the perfect hideout. On the sandy bottom, I see at one point a big flounder, sandy-colored, perfectly blended with the off-white seabed. It moves on its side, never more than a centimeter from the bottom, perfectly camouflaged. Paola notices that evolution has caused both eyes to be on the same side of the body, as the left side is always flat against the sand.

This is what Paola likes. Quality time together. Unhurried. Relaxed. Just the two of us. Nothing crazy. No big feats. Normal, or even slowish, pace. Not even that much talking sometimes. Just closeness.

At 7pm we have a van pick us up from the Sofitel to go to dinner. The restaurant Paola chose is called Kaveka, in Cook's Bay, about 15 minutes by car. A kind man picks us up. The music playing in the van is French, so we all think he is French. He must be about our age.

The lady who greets us at the restaurant is dark-eyed and dark-skinned, wearing a simple dress, her dark hair in a short ponytail. I ask for us to be seated maybe near the water, as we read this is one of the nice options in the restaurant. Andrea and Pietro are as usual fooling around, as she seems to be a bit tentative about where to sit us. Andrea and Pietro in Italian joke saying facetiously, "There is no place for us to sit," while the restaurant instead is only about at most 20% full.

She turns around and says, "Ah, siete italiani?" Now Andrea and Pietro quiet down. She is Italian!! She is a supernice girl from Vicenza, in the Venetian region, north-eastern Italy. She sits us near the water. Her name is Sofia. And she starts chatting away with us.

What a fascinating story she has for us. We learn her father is from Vietnam, but left her family in Italy when she was only six months old. It does not seem like she has had contact with him anymore. Now that we look at her, one can retrospectively guess her eyes are a tiny bit slanted like an Asian, but really she does not look Asian. She states her older sister looks Asian, while she herself looks like her Italian mother.

She has been living in French Polynesia for about four years. She works there in the hotel Kaveka, at the reception in the afternoon and in the evening in the restaurant. She has a ready smile, sweet eyes. She pays only $400 for rent of a house, with two rooms, kitchen, a large yard, not too well kept, she says, but electricity and water are not only present but included in the rent. She has solar panels, as we saw on top of many houses in this trip.

As she returns between appetizer and main course, Sofia tells us she is completely integrated, as she even has a Polynesian boyfriend. She likes him, but says Polynesian families are too close. He still lives with his father, mother, and two sisters. Only the father and her boyfriend, a contractor, work. His sisters are fat and sit home doing nothing. Only one member of the family is supposed to work and take care of the others in Polynesia. Sofia is not too happy about this.

In fact, she herself would be expected to move in with her boyfriend's family. But she says she does not want to. She actually feels bad her boyfriend often has to give money to his lazy sisters. Sofia herself has had to give money to members of her boyfriend's family. She obviously, and rightly so, thinks this is unfair.

As a European, with her Italian passport, she makes us understand that it has been easy for her to work and live permanently in French Polynesia. There are only a few downsides. The language, Tahitian, is very difficult, she says. There seem to be very few words in the vocabulary, but no structure to the language. To say, for example, "The dog got out of the house and barked at the neighbor," Tahitians say, "Dog house neighbor." Or something similar, very basic.

Tahitian belongs to the group of Polynesians languages that include Samoan, Maori, Hawaiian, Rarotongan, and Tongan. There are many different dialects in French Polynesians, almost as many as there are inhabited islands.

She also misses doing a variety of things in Italy, like going to the mountains, or to a movie, or to the countryside, or to a museum. Here one can really just go to the beach, she says. She states she sees very few Italians in her resort. There are a few more at the Sofitel (we had not met any).

She goes to Italy every other year, and has had few people coming to visit her, her parents only once. Her sister has three kids, and she has not met the youngest one, who was just born earlier this month. One can guess she is ready to have kids of her own. She is nice and deserves them.

I have the typical fish soup for appetizer. Not as good as at the Mahogany the night before, but decent. Andrea has a hamburger for appetizer! Pietro a French onion soup. Paola nothing. For second course, Paola has some chicken with Tahitian sauce; Pietro a hamburger; Andrea and I the mahi-mahi. It's pretty good, even if a bit dry.

Sofia is very nice, and stays keeping us company. She says she has not spoken Italian in some time. She has taught some Italian to her boyfriend, the basic words, like "ti amo," (I love you), etc. She says it took her a month to learn to say I love you in Tahitian: Wahere Iao Oe'. At least this is phonetically what I hear, and write on a paper napkin. It translates to "My heart from me to you." Beautiful, I think.

At the end we have become friends. Thinking I'll for sure put her in the book, I ask for her email. She still has an Italian email address, sofiakieu@yahoo.it She makes sure we understand all the letters in her name are small font. Kieu is her Vietnamese last name. She is so excited to give her email to us!!

The same man who drove us here is waiting in front of the restaurant to take us back to the Sofitel. He is really nice. I strike a conversation with him too. He is actually not French, despite the music he was listening to earlier. He is from New Zealand. His grandmother was Tahitian, so he has also a French passport, and can live and work in French Polynesia. He says there are only a couple of New Zealanders in Moorea. He clearly loves it here, and has two kids.

March 29, 2016

I wake up feeling burned. All that time yesterday playing in the lagoon, volleyball, soccer, Tahitian canoeing, has killed my skin. For the first time I did not wear any sunscreen, thinking by now I would have been ready for some direct sun. But the sun here in the South Pacific is super-strong, we are very close to the equator. I should have known better.

Andrea goes running, I should have gone with him, but I'm too afraid of the sun, already bright and stinging at 7am. So we gather ourselves, and we make it another all-you-can-barf, gorgeous, abundant Polynesian breakfast at the Sofitel. Our last. I must admit that being our last day, I'm not only feeling sorry for myself and my skin, but also feeling sad about leaving paradise.

Back at our royal bungalow, Paola and I go for a swim in the lagoon below our room. One can never get tired of seeing these beautiful corals, and especially the fish. Striped black and white, cream colored, small ones of a very light blue hue moving like sperm, some painted with geometric designs and many different colors, some reddish ones.

One of the largest ones, in the shade right under a bungalow, about a foot and a half long, is robust, light brown with white polka dots, and moves using very flimsy light fins. Beautiful. Despite being covered in sun lotion, and being in the water, I feel the sun hitting me. So I get out of the water before Paola. Unheard of.

I take a nice shower, and finish gathering my things. Soon it's 11am, and our luggage gets picked up. I do the check out. Then punctual, even a few minutes early, our taxi arrives.

At the Vaitape ferry terminal, we buy our four tickets for Pape'ete, Tahiti. While we wait, Pietro and I have great fruit juices: a Polynesian local just throws fruits in a blender, and makes a large glass of mango for Pietro, and a mix of mango, banana, pineapple and orange for me. They are delicious.

Andrea, who is always cautious and careful like Paola, watches us drink for a while. When it's clear we are not dying yet of salmonella or some other disease, he orders himself a pineapple and banana one. His is delicious, too. The fluids are what the doctor ordered in this heat!

The ferry arrives a bit late, deposits a few dozens passengers coming from Tahiti, and is soon ready to take us all on. We take off maybe 20 minutes later than the scheduled 12:15pm departure, but mine is a wild guess: who cares about being on time anymore?

We sit together in the upper deck, inside. I soon discover one can step outside, and go to the front open deck of the large metal ferry. I have a great ride, staying here outside the whole time. The distance between Moorea and Pape'ete is less than 20km of blue Pacific waters. The views are spectacular, as we get closer to Tahiti.

I think how lucky I am. What a great life I continue to have. Am I the luckiest person in world? The answer is yes, of course. I have Tahiti in front of me, can you believe it? Wow. I'm in flow, again, enjoying every moment. As we gather speed, now in open waters, wind blows through me. My hat tries multiple times to fly off my head, and I have to keep its cord tightly. I'm probably getting burned again by the sun, right above me. But the view is worth it, and the strong wind does not make me feel the sun much.

Tahiti was not the first of the Society Islands to be populated, as this award goes to Raiatea, more important politically in early modern Polynesian history compared to the bigger Tahiti. Now Tahiti has over 70% of the entire population of French Polynesia, at about 185,000.

Tahiti is made up of two circles connected by a narrow isthmus. The larger north-west circle is Tahiti Nui (Big Tahiti), and the smaller south-east circle is Tahiti Iti (Little Tahiti). These circles are both large craters. In Tahiti Nui, the highest peak of the crater is Mt Orohena, and impressive 2241 meters.

Tahiti's capital Pape'ete means as a Polynesian name 'basket of water.' This name probably derives from the fact that there where water springs here where people came to collect the precious fluid.

The famed and stunning atoll of Tetiaroa is 59km north of Tahiti. Here Marlon Brando came to live – after buying it – with his new love, Tarita Teriipia, his Tahitian co-star in the 1965 classic Mutiny on the Bounty.

We arrive in the main port of Tahiti and French Polynesia, Pape'ete. A real modern and large harbor this time. As we come off, easily and with no wait, I ask the way to our hotel, the Sarah Nui (nui again means 'big'). It's super hot. A policeman-looking guard says it's really close, we have to turn left, then take the first right at the runaround, and then we'll see the hotel on the left side of the street.

It must be over 100 degrees, with melanoma-causing sun strength, but we soon make it to the Sarah Nui, which is about 10 stories high. The first building over one floor we see in Polynesia. There is a line at the hotel, but when we get to the counter the lady is nice.

Room 321 is just being prepared as we get to it, so we wait a few more minutes outside as two busy and quick maids fix the linens and the room in general. Once in, I figure out the air-conditioning does not work. It's very hot in the room, which has two queen beds. I step again outside looking for the maids.

Soon a repairman comes, and fixes the air-conditioning. Later he has to come back when I take the key out of the room slot, and this turns the air-conditioning off, without it coming back on again when I insert the key back in. Once repaired again, I get another key from the front desk so we can leave the air-conditioning on, without touching it anymore!!

By 2:30pm or so, we venture out. It's sunny, scorching hot. Andrea and Pietro are hungry. We go to the market, called Marche' de Pape'ete. It is the most famous attraction in town.

There are probably a hundred stands, and dozens of simple shops, in two large floors covering an entire city block.

Coconuts, tropical fruits, vegetables, fish of all kinds, jams, flowers, tourist attractions such as small dancing dolls or bottled shells, and hundreds of other simple goods are sold in the open stands. I finally see how a breadfruit (uru) and a taro (a tuber, or root vegetable, in the potato family) look like. The shops sell mostly clothing, such as pareu (sarongs), t-shirts, colorful women dresses, woven hats, as well as jewelry, mostly made of corals and dark pearls.

Andrea buys a present − some jam − for his wonderful girlfriend Alice. A few minutes later, he also buys some coco and strawberry ice-cream on a cone. The coco flavor is so good. So I buy another cone, just coco, and give it to Paola. As she happily accepts the gift, then I buy a third one for myself. The lady who sells the ice-cream is smiling away, amused!!

We go around shopping a bit more in the market. Andrea buys another gift for Alice, a tiny Polynesian dress, good at most for a neonate. It's a joke between them that he gets her small children things. I buy a simple neckless made up of a black pearl and a white coral flower for Paola. She adores this stuff, and it looks so good on her.

Pape'ete is no large metropolis. There is not that much around the port. It's really a medium-size town, the only one we see with buildings not only a few stories high, but also sometimes of cement. There are still plenty of shanty dwellings if one veers off the center a bit.

Pape'ete was in fact populated by less than 500 people as recently as 1900. Then the whaling industry and the easy port made it the preferred city to work and live in, and where the Polynesian kings and queens moved to.

At 4pm we are to meet the Schwartz's at the Pape'ete Cathedral, close to the market and still in the small center city area. It's kind of a small church, all open, simple. Cathedrale Notre Dame was completed relatively recently for a church, in 1875. I pray a bit thanking God. I also sit near an open large door, where there is a bit of a breeze. It's still superhot outside.

After the Schwartz's arrive, we all walk around. First we head back to the market to show it to them. They buy some gifts. I buy some chocolates for work. Then we go to a nearby bar along the seaside, where we each get something to drink. As I'm the usual pig, and as I'm feeling a bit dizzy – maybe the heat - I also get a mahi-mahi sandwich.

A few minutes before 6pm, we all take a stroll along the port. There are beautiful ships, including sailing boats. We pass by a touching memorial. It is for the victims of nuclear testing, those here in French Polynesia, as well as others around the world. We all eight read the captions and the names of Polynesian Islands and other international places in gripping silence. Later, as we walk, the harbor looks stunning in the sunset colors. We pass back by the bar place because I had forgotten my hat there ☺.

We walk to L'O a' la bouche restaurant, on Passage Cardella, a small street we have minimal trouble to find. Lori had made 7pm reservations. It is excellent. The first and only air-conditioned restaurant we'll visit in French Polynesia. Pietro and I have duck; it melts in my mouth. Even the sides of vegetables and potatoes are really good. My vanilla cream brulee is good but not great. Andrea's profiterole instead is fantastic.

On our way back, as we go by the ferry port again, we find the legendary mobile food vans of Pape'ete, the roulottes. We watch a bit the crowd scene here, as many people are dining in the open air, and youths bike around only on their back wheel. We buy some bottled water for the night.

March 30, 2016

The dreaded day has arrived. We get the Sarah Nui hotel wake-up call at 4:30am. A few seconds later, my cell phone goes off too. I always have back up. I take the first shower, Andrea the second, Pietro the last. Paola took one last night. I can sense all are fine, in as good a mood one can be leaving paradise this early in the morning. Actually, since is still dark outside, this late at night, I should say.

We have pre-packed the night before. So we are ready quickly. I can still fit into my tight cotton pants, and slim fit shirt. Barely! The hotel room phone goes off at 4:51am. Our taxi is already here, waiting for us. In a minute we line up and get out of the room. At the check-out, I just leave the room keys, and I'm done in a second.

We feel bad as we pass in front of a dozen other people, waiting for the shuttle there before 5am, and climb in a confortable air-conditioned van, all for us. I'm so happy when the Polynesian large lady who drives the taxi says she is indeed for '321' (in French), our room number. Exactly ten minutes (5km west of the city) and 3000 CFPs later (the shuttle would have cost us 4500 CFPs), we are already at the airport.

Faa'a airport in Pape'ete, Tahiti, is unlike any other airport I have ever seen. It's mostly open air. The check-in is done outside. The weather I guess permits it, all year long. It's only 5:10am, so there is only a short line. Later the Schwartz's will be in line for quite a while, but we are lucky and get through security quickly.

Even the international lounge where the gates are is not only small for an international airport, but also open on one side!! There is not really much air-conditioning, and the high temperature is just bearable, as we begin to see the sky getting lighter. There is only one small bar, where we buy the only chocolate croissant available, and three almond croissants. We devour them quickly. Then we have a wait, as the plane is scheduled to leave at 7:35am. The Schwartz's arrive at around 6:45am, having Pietro worried.

As we get through the gate, and out on the runway where the big Air France jet (yes!! no more propeller planes ☺) is waiting for us, I do scream, "I do not want to go! I do not want to go!!" The Polynesian lady showing us the way is laughing, as are the members of my beloved traveling group.

The plane again is full of French people, as this Air France flight will go eventually to Charles-de-Galles, Paris' airport, after landing us in Los Angeles. It's pretty full. We Berghella's are sitting all together in row 39. Soon Pietro and Gabby find a way to sit together.

We fly for almost eight hours over the Pacific Ocean. If one stops and thinks about it, it's pretty scary, as there is really nowhere to do an emergency landing along the route. We have the usual mild turbulence, but nothing much. The lunch they serve is spectacular for airplane food. I can still taste Polynesia in the fish dish they serve. It's – you guess it – in coconut sauce, and probably mahi-mahi. I take an occasional nap, but mostly I am in flow while working on this book on my loved laptop.

Close to the end of the great flight, I go bother Gabby and Pietro, who are sitting close together. They have been talking and touching each other nonstop, it seems. I joke that I'm a steward, and I'm there to congratulate them on their honeymoon. I offer champagne, and caviar. I ask Gabby if she likes her caviar red or black. She says, "Black, of course." We are all smiling.

Once in LA, we go through the many check-outs and check-back-ins. We have dinner together; actually Andrea and Pietro have two dinners, as they each order a burger, and then in another restaurant also quesadillas. They are insatiable. We are getting all tired, and plan to sleep on the 10:15pm red-eye from LA back to Philadelphia. I know the dreams will be good.

Acknowledgments

My trip companions: Paola Luzi, Andrea Berghella, Pietro Berghella, Lori Olson, Henry Schwartz, Jacob (Jake) Schwartz, and Gabrielle (Gabby) Schwartz.

www.ingramcontent.com/pod-product-compliance
Lightning Source LLC
LaVergne TN
LVHW011337080426
835513LV00006B/394